WHEN PAST AND PRESENT MEET
A Companion to
the Study of Christian Thought

Douglas E. Brown, Jr.

PEABODY, MASSACHUSETTS 01961-3473

*To my parents
whose example of faith and hope compels the exploration
of Christian thought*

Substantial portions of chapter four appeared in *Restoration Quarterly* 28 (First Quarter, 1985/86):1-10. Chapter three is forthcoming in the same journal. The material is reprinted by permission from *Restoration Quarterly*.

Table of Contents

Foreword

Reading this book will not take long, but it may send you on a long journey in the study of Christian thought. Although I've spent nearly thirty years exploring the field, as I read, I felt an urge to pull some volumes from my shelves and take a fresh look at the array of ideas Christians have put forth in nearly two millennia of their history.

The study of the history of Christian thought or doctrine often does not sound fascinating to collegians and seminarians attuned more to the present and worried more about the future than the past. Yet under the tutelage of this gifted young teacher, Associate Professor of Christian Doctrine at the Harding Graduate School of Religion in Memphis, it comes alive in both present and future tenses.

This book, you see, is not a history of doctrine. There are plenty of those on the market. It is, rather, a case for the study of the history of Christian thought—an apology, if you will, showing what this discipline can contribute to Christian growth and ministry. Professor Brown argues with clarity and cogency that the study of doctrine, entered into with maturity, can refresh faith, deepen self-examination, broaden fellowship, enrich the study of the Scriptures, and bring balance to theological reflection.

This book is a teacher's friend. As a companion beamed especially toward beginners, it begins, continues, and ends with well-framed questions. In an introduction and four brief but carefully documented chapters, Professor Brown entices us with such questions as: What is the history of doctrine? Why study it? How do I approach the study? What attitudes should I bring to it? What preparation must I have for it?

You will find some of his answers to these questions particularly engaging. Professor Brown's analyses of the various movements within Christian history, including his own (Churches of Christ), are at times critical but always constructive. Readers from rationalistic backgrounds, whether more conservative or liberal, are drawn toward the line of the great "feelers"—Augustine and Pascal and Kierkegaard and Merton—among the thinkers. Readers unacquainted with the richness of Christian thought outside their own heritage are prodded to rediscover the common faith and hope that has united the generations of Christian history. Indeed, one of the most significant features of this fine book may be the section in which the author wrestles with what kind of unity we should seek.

Professor Brown has a gift for simple, apt illustrations. Writing in a style which persons of varying levels of education can appreciate, he renders an immense service to students of theology. Novices will sense the vitality and significance of the history of Christian thought. Experts will find further food for their own reflection in notes. I confidently commend this handbook as an introduction to the field.

E. Glenn Hinson
David T. Porter Professor
  of Church History
The Southern Baptist
  Theological Seminary
Louisville, Kentucky

Acknowledgments

The seeds for this book's production were planted by my first assignments as an undergraduate religion major in 1969. Those seeds have now been nurtured by several years of research, teaching, and experience. These reflections began to take shape in 1979 as oral, and later transcribed, lecture material in historical theology courses. Student interest was such that the price of rewriting has been paid in order to achieve the wider circulation this book permits.

I am indebted to the many persons in Christian history who have, in a sense, become friends and fellow strugglers and also to scores of fellow students who have benefited me by their special expertise with various parts of the story. Only a general thank you can be offered. However, I wish to express special appreciation to several whose insights and criticisms have helped shape these chapters. The history and theology departments at Southern Baptist Theological Seminary provided a challenging training program. The supervision and example of Dr. Glenn Hinson were particularly inspiring. The tutelage of St. Meinrad Professor Cyprian Davis and Oxford Professor Barrington White broadened my cultural and religious sensitivities. My colleagues and students at Harding Graduate School of Religion have allowed me to participate in a rewarding community of inquiry and service. Annie Mae Lewis, Bonnie Baker, and Steve Brown graciously reviewed various drafts of the manuscript. Jean Saunders and more recently Barbara McKinney have given invaluable secretarial assistance. My family has tolerated the time writing consumes and furnished refreshment at low points.

For all of these people, I have the deepest gratitude.

Introduction

Statement of Purpose

What happens in a historical study of Christian thought?[1]
What does it involve? Certainly university and seminary students of religion ask such questions. But so do a variety of
other students of Christian thought from throughout the
Christian population. Even specialists need to return regularly
to these questions. Perhaps the expected answer would describe library searches, reading tasks, assimilation of facts, and
field trips. Tests and research projects would be added to this
description for university and seminary students. Such an answer would be accurate, but would it be complete? I think not.
This answer would be no more sufficient than the impression
that the essence of mastering the piano has to do with
keyboards and pedals, notes and measures.

Beyond the mechanics of a historical study of Christian
thought lies an experience. This means that the questions with
which we began should at some point be answered in terms of
the devotional impact and ministerial value a historical study
of Christian thought can have. What one does (mechanics)
mediates what happens (experience). What happens (experience) gives meaning to what one does (mechanics). Alex
Haley's *Roots* became a media event in part because the audience found the sense of discovery that occurs when past and
present meet. Similarly, when past and present meet in a historical study of Christian thought, the result can be not only
intellectually stimulating but also spiritually rewarding.

Why, then, do so many apparently fail to taste this experience? I think the answer is traced back to responses to the following questions. How can a person complete twelve or even

sixteen years of formal education and possess little "sense of history" or ability to think historically? How can a thirteen-year-old identify ancient history as "before TV"? Why are we so puzzled by an Oxford student who, when asked where he began his reading of modern history, responded "Rome"? Historical amnesia[2] is certainly not unique to Americans. The ancient sage of Ecclesiastes saw this phenomenon as the cause of the common misconception that newness could exist "under the sun" (Eccl. 1:1–11). However, many Americans seem to be especially afflicted by this malady.

No doubt several factors contribute to confusion or doubt about the value of historical research for understanding Christianity. Consider two such factors, each presented with the awareness that exceptions exist to the points being made.

One major factor is that for some, previous schooling has placed comparatively little importance on developing a historical consciousness. Such persons continue to have their "sense of history" limited by our society's "new world" vision brought by the first settlers from Europe, which not surprisingly marked then as well as now the beginning of "relevant" history with American colonization.[3] They likely have followed the crowd in taking a pragmatic "how can I get ahead" motivation for education, an attitude which has left liberal arts repeatedly overshadowed by scientific and technological disciplines.[4] They are no doubt well aware of the rapid changes in American life which make the past seem out of touch with or disconnected from the present and, therefore, the future.[5] They usually have known only a "dates and places" teaching method, which in itself failed to expose the substance of history. Any one or combination of such educational experiences partially accounts for their largely uncultivated historical consciousness.

A second factor, frequently accompanying this educational shortcoming, is the opinion about and interpretations of Christian history many receive from the religious orientation passed on to them. This legacy varies from one religious group to another. Perhaps an illustration will make this point clear. I am associated with Churches of Christ, one facet of a religious movement that emerged in the early 1800s on the American frontier advocating "reformation" or "restoration."[6] Breathing the "new start" atmosphere of the frontier, early participants committed themselves to peeling away from

Christian faith the layers they believed had collected since apostolic days. This "roll back" was expected to initiate the uniting of believers in Christ. Widespread millenarian hope buoyed this expectation. Some leaders of this movement believed they had found in a "reasonable" approach to religion the key to filling out a golden age-apostasy-restoration model for interpreting Christian history. Scientific historiography, at the time embryonic in the United States, had little initial influence within this movement. This analysis could be expanded, but "the bottom line" is this: such factors as these combined to establish points of view toward the interpretation of historical theology that have been passed on to subsequent generations within this heritage. Those studying the history of Christian thought should take the time to determine how their religious heritage has shaped their views of historical research.

In the family classic *Mary Poppins*, the magical nanny changed the Banks children's attitude toward cleaning their room by explaining her theory that "a spoonful of sugar helps the medicine go down." This book has been written to be the "spoonful of sugar" that helps convert a historical approach to Christian thought into a rewarding experience.

Summary of Chapters

Frequently, beginners possess little exposure to the history of Christian life and thought outside their own niche. On occasion they have even been explicitly warned against such exposure. This "caution signal" is like an actual signal that used to flash at drivers negotiating the dangerous "Spaghetti Junction" in Louisville, Kentucky. Drivers saw a sign that said, "When this sign is flashing, you are going too fast." Once a lawyer, approaching the junction early one morning when there was no traffic, noticed from a distance that even when no cars were on the ramp, the sign was flashing! The message—any speed was too fast. Those who receive such a message about historical theology are understandably nervous.

In response to such apprehension about studying historical theology, a justification for and integration of such studies with the purposes of Christian devotion and ministry is offered in chapter 1. Three reasons why this historical study is important are discussed. First, appreciation for Christianity as a historical religion can be deepened. Second, personal thought and practice can be critically appraised in light of the efforts of others who have dealt with similar circumstances. Third, understanding of self and others can be improved.

Agreement on the significance of this study leads to a second concern created by a historical study of Christian thought: How should this inquiry be conducted? To wander without methodological guidelines into the field of historical study is analogous to the experience of many tourists who anticipate great fishing when they journey to the nationally famous Kentucky Lake. Apart from a guide or some basic information, they become disappointed fishermen. Their frustration is compounded as they observe others in cars with local license tags driving away with impressive catches. The difference? The locals catch the fish because, frequently remembering the lay of the land in the pre-lake days, they know what bait to use, how deep the water is, where the brush is, and where the creek beds are. In the same way, initial efforts to study theological history often expose an uncertainty about the conduct of historical research which limits the value derived from the study.

In response to this uncertainty about how to study historical theology, suggestions about historical methodology are offered in chapter 2. First, a survey of approaches adopted over the years of Christian history to this type of study is provided in order to highlight movements in Christians' interpretation of their heritage and to demonstrate the time-boundness of methods for studying historical theology. Second, this survey is followed by recommendations concerning the aim and tools needed for a useful study of Christian thought. Finally, four basic principles are introduced as methodological guidelines for the study of Christian thought.

Those who take their excursions into historical theology seriously will face questions crucial to their devotional life. One of the most frequent devotional concerns stirred by the study of historical theology has to do with the unity and divisions among fellow confessors of Christian faith. Alongside the actual study, they are left to wonder: How should I view my own Christian heritage which has been shown to have both strengths and weaknesses? How should I regard those believers outside my particular religious heritage with whom the study of historical theology has acquainted me?

An analysis of the roads more and less traveled by those wrestling with the problem of unity and diversity among followers of Christ is offered in chapter 3. The general comments given here should by all means be accompanied by more specific and personal counsel from an advisor who shares each questioner's heritage and who is sensitive to these problems.

The thesis undergirding all of these reflections is that the study of historical theology can make a significant contribution to Christian ministry. However, acceptance of this thesis (chapter 1) and use of a constructive methodology (chapter 2) do not guarantee this result. Spiritual maturity will make the difference. When in the throes of what Helmut Thielicke has called "theological puberty,"[7] those studying the history of Christian thought may, by gaining such exposure, even be initially made less effective for serving others.

Counsel is given in chapter 4 about the maturity necessary before acquaintance with historical theology can be beneficial to Christian ministry. First, signs of a more adolescent handling of some introduction to historical theology are discussed. Second, indications of passing through this adolescence to spiritual maturity are suggested.

A Final Note to the Reader

Since these "conversations" with those studying the theology in Christian history are limited to supplying points of departure for engaging in such studies, suggestions for further discussion are included at the end of each chapter. Also, several representatives of the points of view being discussed are mentioned in the chapter endnotes. The value of these notes will be proportional to one's familiarity with Christian history. Those who have had little exposure to historical theology should not be discouraged by their lack of familiarity with many of the persons mentioned. Still, these specific references should create a real-life impression about historical theology and perhaps help in locating a few persons about whom to read more. If these chapters are periodically reread, the value of these references will increase.

Further Discussion

1. What are your feelings about the relationship of historical study and Christian ministry?

2. How would you assess the "sense of history" your education has given you?

3. Review your courses and reading in religious as well as general history in order to identify what strengths and weaknesses you bring to your present studies.

4. How receptive is your religious heritage to inquiry into historical theology?

5. How do you expect your historical studies to be conducted?

NOTES

[1]Human beings are distinguished from other creatures at least in the fact that, beyond instinctive reaction to circumstances, human beings have the course of their existence shaped by efforts to live out their judgments about the meaning or purpose of existence. Thought about these judgments is distinctly "theological" when the reference point is ultimately "God," i.e., reality or being believed to be beyond human beings and the natural environment. Theological thought is distinctly "Christian" when such thought can be adequately accounted for only by reference to the essential influence of Jesus Christ. "History of Christian thought" (and related phrases) includes all attempts known to have been made to explain the living hope toward meaningful existence that is believed to originate in Jesus Christ. In this volume, attention is primarily focused on the history of Christian thought subsequent to apostolic times.

[2]Friedrich Nietzsche, in *The Use and Abuse of History*, trans. Adrian Collins (Indianapolis: Bobbs-Merrill Co., 1957), p. 5, pointed to the unaware beast of the field as a symbol of historical amnesia.

[3]Works such as Dee Alexander Brown's *Bury My Heart at Wounded Knee: An Indian History of the American West* (New York: Holt, Rinehart & Winston, 1970), demonstrate how the history of those who had long inhabited this land has been treated as relatively worthless by the more recent, European settlers. See also Perry Miller, *The New England Mind: The Seventeenth Century* (Cambridge: Harvard University Press, 1954), and Henry Farnham May, *The Enlightenment in America* (New York: Oxford University Press, 1976), for insight into the way religious and philosophical commitments to a "new world" so

truncated the boundaries of relevant history as to create this historical amnesia.

[4]William J. Bennett, *To Reclaim a Legacy: A Report on the Humanities in Higher Education* (Washington, D.C.: National Endowment for the Humanities, 1984). For theological commentary on this situation, see E. Glenn Hinson, *A Serious Call to a Contemplative Lifestyle* (Philadelphia: Westminster, 1974); Pierre Teilhard de Chardin, *The Divine Milieu* (New York: Harper & Row, 1960); and Thomas Merton, *Conjectures of a Guilty Bystander* (Garden City, N.Y.: Doubleday & Co., 1968).

The practical importance of scientific and technological disciplines is not being overlooked. However, an educational philosophy that rapidly expands the acquisition of scientific knowledge and the development of technology without giving primary attention to cultural roots and moral maturity makes for a most precarious time. The disturbing gap that presently exists between medical technology and social ethics clearly demonstrates this uneven educational philosophy.

[5]See Alvin Toffler, *Future Shock* (New York: Bantam Books, 1970); Toffler, *The Third Wave* (New York: Bantam Books, 1980); and John Naisbitt, *Megatrends: Ten New Directions Transforming Our Lives* (New York: Warner Books, 1982).

[6]For a thorough treatment of this movement's beginnings, see Earl Irvin West, *The Search for the Ancient Order: A History of the Restoration Movement, 1849–1906*, 2 vols. (Nashville: Gospel Advocate Co., 1949).

[7]Helmut Thielicke, *A Little Exercise for Young Theologians*, trans. Charles L. Taylor (Grand Rapids, Mich.: Eerdmans, 1972), p. 12.

1 *Why Am I Doing This?*

I DO NOT REMEMBER tackling this question during high school or university history courses. While enjoying such courses, I suppose I did not take education seriously enough to see the importance of such a question as, Why am I doing this? Does this sound familiar? However, early in my graduate training, several peers and I openly questioned the relevance of historical study for Christian living. The question has remained to this day. After several years of teaching historical theology, I am certain my early experience was not exceptional. Apparently many wander into the literature from the history of Christian thought without any rationale to guide them.

In the following paragraphs, three responses to the question, Why am I doing this? are discussed. No doubt other responses could be given, but these have become more and more important for me. Discovering answers to the question *why* not only justifies historical studies, but also clarifies how to take notes, what research projects to choose, and what questions to ask.

Appreciation for Christianity as a Historical Religion Can Be Deepened

A first and perhaps most basic reason historical studies can contribute to Christian ministry has to do with the identity of the Christian religion. Those participating in the study of historical theology bring with them a point of view concerning the identity of Christian faith and ministry. Fundamental to this volume is the view that the Christian religion is essentially historical.[1] Accordingly, the Christian message concerns the experience of reconciliation in and beyond history, but not independent of history. This reconciliation has two points of focus, i.e., the initiative of God in bringing about reconciliation and the human experience of reconciliation through response to this initiative. The great commandments Jesus identified as the thrust of "the Law and the Prophets"—the love of God and neighbor (Mt. 22:34–40)—constitute this experience. With the God of Christianity meeting human beings in history, the "always" (truth perceived from God's vantage point) is in part discovered and experienced by human beings interacting with and transforming the "now" (history). Devotional practices (e.g., confession, baptism, prayer, proclamation, and communion) and organizational structures symbolize and in some sense mediate this experience of grace.

Many writers, ancient and modern, have agonized about the apparent lack of meaning in existence and the destiny of history.[2] The first Christians announced a more hopeful outlook. They interpreted their history as the fruition of God's creative work, his liberating the Israelite slaves, his disciplining Israel with Babylonian captivity, his becoming flesh in Jesus of Nazareth, and his raising Jesus from the dead. This "sense of history" sustained them when their faith was threatened (Mt. 5:10–12, Hebrews 11, and 1 Pet. 5:6–11).

Christians outside the predominantly Jewish setting of early apostolic days, however, have faced cultures frequently not so steeped in historical consciousness. In such circumstances, Christians in their efforts evangelistically and theologically to transpose the gospel for new audiences have struggled to maintain a sense of history in their presentation of Christian faith. Consider some illustrations.

Casting Christian thought in a Platonic mold seemed to many early church leaders to be good apologetic and evangelistic strategy. However, this decision also resulted frequently in a modifying of the Jewish and early Christian concept of a personal God active in and affected by human history. Platonic thought located ultimate reality outside time and space in a changeless, spiritual realm. The resulting low view of history, often compounded by an Oriental idea of matter as intrinsically evil, pressured many early Christians to spiritualize their handling of Scripture and their theology. Reflecting this, theologians at the councils of Nicea (325), Constantinople (381), and Chalcedon (451) forged doctrinal resolutions about the Son's relation to the Father and about the divine and human natures of Christ that resulted in a somewhat historically detached concept of God and, therefore, a view of Christ somewhat estranged from the historical Jesus.[3]

This early Christians' struggle to maintain a "sense of history" in their theology was repeated during the post-Reformation, Enlightenment era when many Christians attempted to interpret the Christian faith in terms of its logical or philosophical "reasonableness." At this time, attention was shifting away from the past to present and future interests. Scientifically guided reason came to supersede political, religious, or philosophical authorities in the pursuit of truth. Some concluded universal truth could not be dependent on "the accidents of history."[4] In these circumstances, several religious leaders gave rationalistic apologies for the Christian faith.[5] With God viewed as removed from the flow of history except through the "laws of nature," Christian thought was gradually reduced from an interpretation of history to a discussion of Christian ethics.

Since the late-eighteenth century, several mediating theologies have emerged in the attempt to break away from the effects of such non-historical thinking about the Christian faith without severing ties with modern thought. These efforts have varied from following scientific historical methods[6] to proposing a special religious or salvation history[7] to interpreting God as a participant in the historical processes of becoming and change.[8]

Repeatedly, Christians who join in the task of demonstrating and proclaiming the historical religion of Christ have to deal with pressures within their religious setting to modify or jettison the historical character of the Chrsitian faith. Historical studies will help one deal with such circumstances by deepening a "sense of history," by revealing to what degree the theology passed on has retained the historical character of the faith, and by securing a historically sensitive handling of Scripture in the search for the will of God.

Personal Thought and Practice
Can Be Compared and Critically Appraised

A second reason historical studies can contribute to Christian ministry is their didactic value. Since historical theology has to do with life and thought, this study will become a personal learning experience. A Christian minister shoulders the responsibility of leading those being served in the effort to translate their faith into life today. Historical studies allow them to learn from the attempts of others to fulfill this task.

One major transition faced by early Christians (symbolized by the line between the years AD 50 and 150 in Figure 1–1) came with the passing of the opportunity to appeal directly to apostolic witnesses or to imitate unconditionally the thought and life of the first Christians. This shift occurred early for groups that, by being scattered from Jerusalem (Acts 8), found themselves removed from immediate apostolic supervision. For others this transition was slower. Apostolic letters which provided guidance for struggling churches survive from as late as the turn of the century. It is safe to say that by the mid-second century this transition was behind Christians as they faced theological and ministerial tasks.

FIGURE 1–1

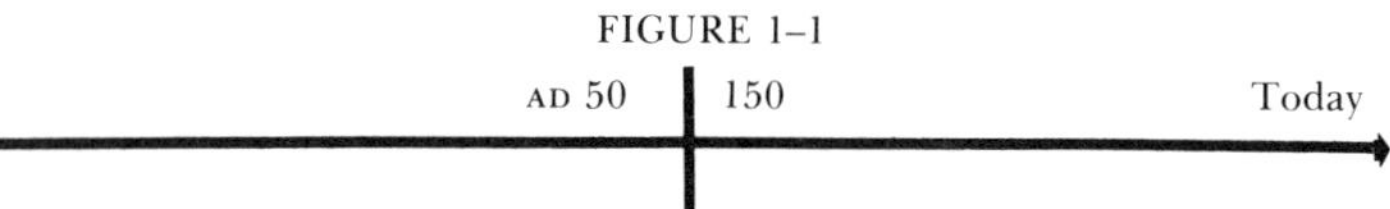

This transition did not strip the apostolic witness of any lasting significance in the history of Christianity. To the contrary, while interpretations have varied, the normative role of apostolic Christianity has continued to be generally acknowledged among Christians. However, this transition has meant that Christians in subsequent generations have had to resolve certain recurring theological and devotional problems not directly treated within the apostolic witness. This is why, in spite of first impressions, a Christian today is in a real sense much nearer to Christians of 150 than those of 50.[9] Historical studies afford the opportunity to test alternatives for dealing with these recurring theological problems. This exposure to the efforts of others will inform and broaden the inquirer's basis for theological decision making. Consider some illustrations of this.

Generations of Christians after apostolic days continue to share *the problem of translating Christian faith into cultures significantly different from its initial setting.* Many among the earliest Christians, loyal to that initial culture, approached their task of propagating a universal gospel cautiously. Paul's ministry forced the issue. By the mid-second century, Christians were not only addressing but were largely coming from predominantly no-Jewish backgrounds. By the late-fourth century, official opposition to the Christian faith had been reversed. Christendom emerged. Church and state weathered several generations during which each party vied for preeminence. However, this uneasy marriage finally began to break down during the transition from medieval feudalism to the modern experiments with democracy, scientific guidance, and religious freedom in Europe and America. When, during this same transition, Western churches spread into African, South American, and Far Eastern countries, Christians faced other radically different cultures.

All such cultural circumstances, ranging in reaction to the Christian faith from indifference to receptivity to hostility, are removed from apostolic Christianity's predominantly Jewish setting in which societal ignorance about Christianity was common. Without direct guidance from the apostolic witness, subsequent generations have had to grapple with several questions concerning the relationship of Christianity and culture. What should our attitude be about adaptability? To what degree should we adapt? What is essential to the identity of Christian faith and, therefore, needs to be carried into different cultural settings? Did primitive Christianity have to cease so that essential Christianity would survive?

As suggested by H. Richard Niebuhr in his *Christ and Culture*,[10] Christians have responded in several ways to these questions. Some have attempted to minimize identification of the Christian faith with a new culture.[11] Some, assessing the addressed culture more positively, have attempted to maximize the common ground with Christian faith.[12] Others have taken a more cautious, prophetic stance before cultures perceived as hostile to Christian faith.[13] Historical studies can test personal thought on these questions by examining the responses of others.

Generations of Christians after apostolic days continue to share the *problem with religious authority*. Many young people experience a rude awakening when they find themselves "on their own." Having depended as teenagers perhaps too much on mom and dad, they abruptly face the disturbing question, How am I going to make decisions now? By analogy, post-apostolic generations quickly began facing this same question.

The issue continues to be not whether the earliest Christian writings have authority, but how that authority is related to *now*. How should Jewish Scripture be used?[14] How does the variety in thought found among the first Christians affect the authority of apostolic writings?[15] What influence should the thought of Christians after apostolic days have? Should appeal be made to philosophy or social sciences in the proclamation and explanation of the gospel?

Beginning soon after apostolic days, people centering their lives on Jesus Christ began exploring several options in dealing with such questions. Montanists argued for a continuing voice of God immediately heard through prophets serving as mouthpieces for the Holy Spirit.[16] Gnostics turned to a more esoteric form of revelation from God, i.e., illumination transferred from Jesus to a special few via an oral tradition of the apostles.[17] Irenaeus pointed to the leadership of apostolically founded churches.[18] In later generations, Eastern Orthodox churches have attempted to find, in Christian thought through the eighth century, solutions to questions about Christian experience and thought that have surfaced between then and now.[19] Roman Catholics have committed themselves to the ongoing decisions of church leaders comprising an authoritative teaching office.[20] Anglicans and Lutherans have experimented with a blend of spiritual and political guidance of Christian experience and thought.[21] Some have tested the idea that each person, if given an opportunity to read the Bible, will sufficiently understand alike what the word from God is for the present.[22] Still others have consciously looked to various philosophies for guidance.[23] Present-day liberation theologians look for analytical help from the social sciences, particularly Marxist interpretations.[24] Historical inquiry can reveal the strengths and weaknesses of these options.

Generations of Christians after apostolic days continue to face searching *questions about God's involvement in history*. Acts of God are reported in Scripture along with records of persistent doubts about the presence of God (Job, Ecclesiastes, Psalms, Habakkuk, and Revelation). Post-apostolic generations have struggled to relate to the providentially active God of Abraham, Isaac, Jacob, Jesus, and the first Christians. Most Christians, from the Roman Empire of early Christian history to the present, have come from cultures where life experiences have been commonly interpreted in terms of supernatural activity. Thus, they have found occasion to "see" the activity of God in their lives. The rise of scientifically guided, Enlightenment societies has brought challenges to the traditional ideas of providence.[25] In response, some have attempted to redefine interpretations of God's activity in light of a scientific focus on natural explanations of events.[26] Others, often through charismatic and healing ministries, have promoted the more traditional view of providence, though at the expense of not integrating scientific advances. Historical inquiry can expose how Christians have handled this serious devotional concern.

Generations of Christians after apostolic days have had to account for *the absence of Christ's return, as expected by the first Christians*. Among them, ethical discussions were frequently couched in such eschatological anticipation (Matthew 24; 1 Corinthians; 1 Peter; Revelation). However, with the passing of time, the promise of Christ's return increasingly became a problem. "Where is the promise of his coming?" (2 Pet. 3:4).

Subsequent generations responded to this question in a variety of ways. Some apparently replaced this linear view of history culminating in Christ's return with a more Platonic and dualistic view of being delivered away from the cyclical realm of time and space.[27] Some repeatedly pushed the date of Christ's return forward, continuing to interpret in their day the "signs" of cultural decay and the impending day of the Lord.[28] The more optimistic Enlightenment mindset led some to interpret the progress of civilization eschatologically[29] and others to push a futurist eschatology to the margins of theological discussion.[30] When the exploitation of industrial expansion and the massive cruelty of World War I revealed that power and greed were guiding modern societies more than enlightened reason, renewed interest in eschatology surfaced. Confidence in a century-long search for the historical Jesus waned because in this impressive effort Jesus had been too radically separated from the eschatological views of his day. What options were left? Some followed Albert Schweitzer in concluding that the Jesus of Palestine held eschatological views which cut him off from the modern setting.[31] Others distinguished between a secular interpretation of history based on scientific methods and a religious interpretation of history rooted in and verified by Christian revelation.[32] Others interpreted eschatology existentially.[33] Still others have pointed to the future of universal history.[34] Historical research can provide important resources for interpreting this common confession and concern about eschatology.

Every interpreter of Scripture and the Christian faith brings a particular point of view to the task. Unwillingness to admit this fact locks in any shortcomings that this limited perspective has. However, once this limitation is admitted, the didactic value that can accompany the study of historical theology becomes obvious. By such study, Christians can more broadly and clearly formulate their thought about matters fundamental to Christian ministry.

Understanding of Self and Others Can Be Improved

With the discussion of these identity-forming and didactic reasons for historical theology studies, this third justification may already be anticipated. When a particular Christian heritage represents the accumulated efforts of several generations, awareness of the sources from which that heritage has sprung understandably becomes blurred. In Joseph Stein's *Fiddler on the Roof*,[35] this problem has been treated in a frequently humorous and yet penetrating way. In his opening dialogue, Tevye, after boasting that the Jewish people of the Russian town Anatevka had a tradition for every circumstance, anticipated the question as to where these traditions originated. His answer: "I'll tell you—I don't know!" As the play continues, the combined pressures of social upheaval on the eve of the Bolshevik revolution and his daughters' bending long-standing traditions forced Tevye to test his traditions. This inbreak of "the new day" led Tevye to understand his traditions better. For instance, reflecting on a particularly agonizing struggle with his daughter Hodel, he wondered, ". . . our old ways were once new, weren't they?"

Questions about the roots of one's Christian heritage are certainly in order, especially when the surrounding cultural circumstances radically change. To what degree are our thoughts and actions rooted in Scripture? How have the efforts of previous generations in relating Christian faith to their times shaped our present thought and practice? Studying historical theology can bring some answers to the "I don't know's" with which one begins. A clear understanding of this background is crucial for each new generation's effort to present the essence of Christianity to the present culture, to encourage Christian fellowship, and to broaden the fuller covenant of brotherhood intended by God for all people.

Studying historical theology also promotes a better understanding of others. Exposure to biographical information and primary source reading will likely create several surprises and also a sensed kinship with those studied. Perhaps a preview is in order.

Frequently, students of Christian thought are surprised to learn that Augustine could make only limited use of Greek in the formation of his thought. That medieval scholasticism introduced an educational method still in use today, i.e., question framing, disputation, and decision making. That Thomas Aquinas, though personally desiring to be "a simple preacher," was viewed as a modernist by many of his peers because of his search for common ground between Christian faith and the newly reintroduced Aristotelian writings. That justification by faith through grace was affirmed at the Roman Catholic Council of Trent (1545–64) as well as by Protestants. That the "liberal" Christianity proposed by the nineteenth-century theologian Friedrich Schleiermacher for modern societies was Christ-centered. That Walter Rauschenbusch did take sin and eschatology seriously in his promotion of a "social gospel." That Harry Emerson Fosdick, twentieth-century popularizer of liberal theology in America, wrote a devotional classic on *The Meaning of Prayer*. That many nineteenth-century predecessors of "fundamentalism" led in social activism in the name of Christ. That Karl Barth, believing that theology and ministry were inseparable, led Christian opposition to Naziism while writing the first volumes of his *Church Dogmatics*. That Rudolf Bultmann presented his celebrated 1941 essay "New Testament and Mythology" to a group of Confessing Church ministers whom he feared were retreating from interaction with current ethical issues. That Reinhold Niebuhr developed his seminal ideas concerning Christian faith and social justice during a dozen years of ministry in Detroit when the automotive industry and the ensuing social problems emerged. That the Catholic Church, in the documents of Vatican II (1962–65), qualified a strictly hierarchical doctrine of the church, encouraged Bible study by scholars and lay persons, admitted partial responsibility for the sixteenth-century divisions, and supported religious freedom.

Such insights into why others in the name of Christ think and act as they do can multiply through the study of historical theology. Though this understanding alone cannot erase all barriers to fellowship among confessors of Christian faith, efforts to promote such fellowship have been found to be more productive when the participants are capable of reviewing both their own heritage and that of others. Divisions caused by factors such as personality clashes, cultural differences, or ignorance can be more easily eliminated. With closer ties, common ground can be confessed and remaining differences can be addressed in less emotionally charged settings.

Conclusion

In August of 1980 I agreed to help my brother move his family from Memphis to Los Angeles on the condition that we would leave I–40 long enough to visit the Grand Canyon. In fact, we zig-zagged north and south of I–40 for the entire trip. We parked near the Grand Canyon on a late afternoon. After exhausting my film supply in a race against the clock, I began walking away satisfied with my photographic achievement. Suddenly, I realized I had gotten pictures capable of jogging my memory about the visit, but I was leaving without the memorable experience about which I had dreamed. Hurriedly, I returned to the Grand Canyon's edge in search of a place to sit quietly in order to hear and see. As the minutes passed, several others had joined in experiencing the wonder of a Grand Canyon sunset.

Too often, inquirers into historical theology leave prematurely. This chapter has pointed to the discovery possible when those studying the history of Christian thought balance their many activities with quiet reflection. I hope by now a convincing, or at least defensible, case has been made for the conviction that studying historical theology can add significantly to Christian growth and ministry. However, benefiting in these and other ways depends upon how this inquiry is conducted. Therefore, the next chapter addresses the question, How am I going to do this?

Further Discussion

1. Does your present thought about the Christian faith reflect its historical character?

2. Read Exodus 12; Numbers 9; Deuteronomy 6, 11; Josh. 4:1–7; Psalms 68; 78; Hosea; and Acts 7; 17. How significant should this historical consciousness be for Christian thought?

3. How might a "sense of history" affect Christian practices such as prayer and communion?

4. Do you agree that in certain ways a Christian today has more in common with second-century Christians than with first-century Christians?

5. How should Christianity and culture relate?

6. How would you relate Scripture, post-apostolic theology, and human reason in theological formation?

7. How significant is eschatology to your religious heritage?

8. Do you believe God acts today as he is described as acting in Scripture?

9. Are you willing to put your thought and heritage to the test of historical inquiry?

10. Are you willing to drop preconceived impressions about others that do not square with the discoveries of historical research?

11. Can you think of other values in studying historical theology?

NOTES

[1]C. H. Dodd, *History and the Gospel* (New York: C. Scribner's Sons, 1938); Jürgen Moltmann, *The Crucified God: The Cross of Christ as the Foundation and Criticism of Christian Theology*, trans. R. A. Wilson and

John Bowden (New York: Harper & Row, 1974); John Warwick Montgomery, *The Shape of the Past: A Christian Response to Secular Philosophies of History*, 2d ed. (Minneapolis, Minn.: Bethany Fellowship, 1975); Stephen Neill, *Christian Faith and Other Faiths: The Christian Dialogue with Other Religions*, 2d ed. (London: Oxford University Press, 1970); Wolfhart Pannenberg, ed., *Revelation as History*, trans. David Granskou (New York: Macmillan Co., 1968); Norman Pittenger, *Christian Faith and the Question of History* (Philadelphia: Fortress, 1973); Ralph G. Wilburn, *The Historical Shape of Faith* (Philadelphia: Westminster, 1966); and John Francis Wilson, *Religion: A Preface* (Englewood Cliffs, N.J.: Prentice-Hall, 1982).

[2] Søren Kierkegaard, *The Journals of Søren Kierkegaard*, ed. and trans. Alexander Dru (New York: Oxford University Press, 1938); Fyodor Dostoyevsky, *Notes from Underground* and *The Grand Inquisitor*, trans. Ralph E. Matlaw (New York: E. P. Dutton & Co., 1960); Arthur Schopenhauer, *Essays and Aphorisms*, trans. R. J. Hollingdale (Baltimore, Md.: Penguin Books, 1970); Bertrand Russell, *The Autobiography of Bertrand Russell*, 3 vols. (vols. 1–2, Boston, Mass.: Little, Brown & Co., 1967–68; vol. 3, New York: Simon and Schuster, 1969); and Albert Camus, *The Stranger*, trans. Stuart Gilbert (New York: Random House, 1954).

[3] Aloys Grillmeier, *Christ in Christian Tradition*, 2d rev. ed., trans. John Bowden (Atlanta: John Knox, 1975).

[4] Gotthold Ephraim Lessing, *Lessing's Theological Writings*, ed. and trans. Henry Chadwick (London: Adam & Charles Black, 1956), pp. 51–56.

[5] John Locke, *The Reasonableness of Christianity*, ed. I. T. Ramsey (Stanford, Calif.: Stanford University Press, 1958); Matthew Tindal, *Christianity as Old as Creation* (New York: Garland Publications, 1978); John Toland, *Christianity Not Mysterious* (Ann Arbor, Mich.: University Microfilm, 1978); and Immanuel Kant, *Religion Within the Limits of Reason Alone*, trans. Theodore M. Greene and Hoyt H. Hudson (New York: Harper & Row, 1960).

[6] Friedrich Schleiermacher, *The Christian Faith*, ed. and trans. H. R. Mackintosh and J. S. Steward (Philadelphia: Fortress, 1976); Ernst Troeltsch, *The Absoluteness of Christianity and the History of Religions*, trans. David Reid (Richmond, Va.: John Knox, 1971); and Adolf von Harnack, *What Is Christianity?* trans. Thomas Bailey Saunders (New York: Harper & Row, 1957). For secondary analyses of these approaches, see Walter E. Wyman, Jr., *The Concept of Glaubenslehre: Ernst Troeltsch and the Theological Heritage of Schleiermacher* (Chico, Calif.: Scholars Press, 1983), and Wilhelm Pauck, *Harnack and Troeltsch: Two Historical Theologians* (New York: Oxford University Press, 1968).

[7] Karl Barth, *The Epistle to the Romans*, 6th ed., trans. Edwyn C. Hoskyns (London: Oxford University Press, 1933), and *The Resurrection of the Dead*, trans. H. J. Stenning (London: Hodder & Stoughton, 1933).

[8] Pierre Teilhard de Chardin, *The Phenomenon of Man* (New York: Harper & Row, 1959); Wolfhart Pannenberg, *Jesus: God and Man*, 2d

ed., trans. Lewis L. Wilkins and Duane A. Priebe (Philadelphia: Westminster, 1977); and Ewert H. Cousins, ed., *Process Theology: Basic Writings* (New York: Newman Press, 1971).

[9]Everett Ferguson, *Early Christians Speak* (Austin, Tex.: Sweet Publishing Co., 1971).

[10]H. Richard Niebuhr, *Christ and Culture* (New York: Harper & Row, 1951). See also E. Glenn Hinson, *The Evangelization of the Roman Empire: Identity and Adaptability* (Macon, Ga.: Mercer University Press, 1981).

[11]Tertullian, *Disciplinary, Moral, and Ascetical Works*, trans. Rudolph Arbesmann, Sister Emily Joseph Daly, and Edwin A. Quain (New York: Fathers of the Church, 1959); Leo Tolstoy, *A Confession, The Gospel in Brief, and What I Believe*, trans. Aylmer Maude (London: Oxford University Press, 1940); Anne Fremantle, ed., *The Papal Encyclicals in Their Historical Context* (New York: New American Library, 1963); R. A. Torrey, A. C. Dixon, et al., eds., *The Fundamentals: A Testimony to the Truth*, 12 vols. (Los Angeles: Bible Institute, 1909; reprint ed., Grand Rapids, Mich.: Baker, 1970); and C. Allyn Russell, ed., *Voices of American Fundamentalism: Seven Biographical Studies* (Philadelphia: Westminster, 1976).

[12]Clement of Alexandria, *Exhortation to the Heathen; The Instructor; The Stromata; Who Is the Rich Man Who Shall Be Saved?* Ante-Nicene Fathers, vol. 2 (Grand Rapids, Mich.: Eerdmans, 1975); Peter Abelard, *Christian Theology*, trans. J. Ramsay McCallum (Oxford: Blackwell, 1948); Friedrich Schleiermacher, *On Religion: Speeches to Its Cultured Despisers*, trans. John Oman (New York: Harper & Row, 1958); Walter Rauschenbusch, *Christianizing the Social Order* (New York: Macmillan Co., 1942); Adolf von Harnack and Wilhelm Herrmann, *Essays on the Social Gospel*, trans. G. M. Craik, ed. Maurice A. Canney (New York: G. P. Putnam's Sons, 1907); and Paul Tillich, *Theology of Culture* (New York: Oxford University Press, 1959).

[13]Augustine, *The City of God Against the Pagans*, trans. George E. McCracken (Cambridge: Harvard University Press, 1957–72); John Calvin, *Institutes of the Christian Religion*, 2 vols., trans. Henry Beveridge (Grand Rapids, Mich.: Eerdmans, 1975); Søren Kirekegaard, *Attack Upon Christendom*, trans. Walter Lowrie (Princeton, N.J.: Princeton University Press, 1968); Reinhold Niebuhr, *An Interpretation of Christian Ethics* (New York: Seabury Press, 1979); and Gustavo Gutierrez, *A Theology of Liberation: History, Politics, and Salvation*, ed. and trans. Sister Caridad Inda and John Eagleson (Maryknoll, N.Y.: Orbis Books, 1973).

[14]P. R. Ackroyd and C. F. Evans, eds., *From the Beginnings to Jerome*, vol. 1 of *The Cambridge History of the Bible*, 3 vols. (New York: Cambridge University Press, 1970).

[15]H. E. W. Turner, *The Pattern of Christian Truth: A Study in the Relations Between Orthodoxy and Heresy in the Early Church* (London: Mowbray, 1954); Oscar Cullmann, *The Christology of the New Testament*, rev. ed., trans. Shirley C. Guthrie and Charles A. M. Hall (Philadelphia: Westminster, 1963); and Richard N. Longenecker, *The Christology of Early Jewish Christianity*, reprinted (Grand Rapids: Baker, 1982).

[16]Karl Baus, *From the Apostolic Community to Constantine*, Handbook of Church History, vol. 1 (New York: Herder & Herder, 1965), and *Encyclopedia of Religion and Ethics*, 1955 ed., s.v. "Montanism," by H. J. Lawlor.

[17]James M. Robinson, ed., *The Nag Hammadi Library*, trans. Harold W. Attridge, Hans-Gebhard Bethge, Alexander Böhlig, et al. (New York: Harper & Row, 1977).

[18]Irenaeus, *Against Heresies*, The Ante-Nicene Fathers, vol. 1 (Grand Rapids, Mich.: Eerdmans, 1975).

[19]Georges Florovsky, "Scripture and Tradition: An Orthodox Point of View," *Dialog* 2 (Autumn 1963): 288–93.

[20]*New Catholic Encyclopedia*, 1967 ed., s.v. "Teaching Authority of the Church," by J. R. Lerch; and Francis A. Sullivan, *Magisterium: Teaching Authority in the Catholic Church* (Ramsey, N.J.: Paulist Press, 1984).

[21]Hajo Holborn, *The Reformation*, vol. 1 of *A History of Modern Germany*, (London: Eyre & Spottiswoode, 1965); Erwin Iserloh, Joseph Glazik, and Hubert Jedin, *Reformation and Counter Reformation*, vol. 5 of *History of the Church*, trans. Anselm Biggs and Peter W. Becker (New York: Seabury Press, 1980); Ernst Christian Helmreich, *The German Churches under Hitler: Background, Struggle, and Epilogue* (Detroit: Wayne State University Press, 1980); Robert K. Faulkner, *Richard Hooker and the Politics of a Christian England* (Berkeley: University of California Press, 1981); Olive J. Brose, *Church and Parliament: The Reshaping of the Church of England, 1828–1860* (Stanford, Calif.: Stanford University Press, 1959); and William Temple, *Christianity and the State* (London: Macmillan & Co., 1928).

[22]Erasmus, a sixteenth-century Christian and humanist, represents the groundswell of confidence in human beings existing by his time. The vision that access to Scripture and education could usher in much needed reform has captured the imaginations of many, as Enlightenment changes in the social order and the proliferation of Bible societies for the translation and distribution of Scripture indicate. For an introduction to Erasmus, see Johan Huizinga, *Erasmus and the Age of Reformation*, trans. F. Hopman and Barbara Flower (New York: Harper & Row, 1957).

[23]Origen, *On First Principles*, trans. G. W. Butterworth (Gloucester, Mass.: Peter Smith, 1973); Augustine, *Confessions*, trans. Vernon J. Bourke (New York: Fathers of the Church, 1953); Thomas Aquinas, *Summa Theologiae*, trans. Thomas Gilby, Timothy McDermott, Herbert McCabe, et al. (New York: McGraw-Hill, 1964–81); G. W. F. Hegel, *On Art, Religion, Philosophy: Introductory Lectures to the Realm of Absolute Spirit*, ed. J. Glenn Gray, trans. Bernard Bosanquet, E. B. Speirs, J. Burdon Sanderson, et al. (New York: Harper & Row, 1970); Paul Tillich, *Systematic Theology*, vol. 1 (Chicago: University of Chicago Press, 1951); Rudolf Bultmann, "New Testament and Mythology," in *Kerygma and Myth: A Theological Debate*, ed. Hans-Werner Bartsch, trans. Reginald H. Fuller (London: SPCK, 1953); and Ewert H. Cousins, ed., *Process Theology: Basic Writings* (New York: Newman Press, 1971). For secondary studies, see Colin Brown, *Philosophy and the Christian Faith* (Downer's Grove, Ill.:

Inter-Varsity Press, 1968), and John Macquarrie, *Twentieth-Century Religious Thought: The Frontiers of Philosophy and Theology, 1900–1970*, rev. ed. (London: SCM Press, 1971).

[24]James H. Cone, *A Black Theology of Liberation* (Philadelphia: J. B. Lippincott Co., 1970); Jose Miranda, *Marx and the Bible: A Critique of the Philosophy of Oppression*, trans. John Eagleson (Maryknoll, N.Y.: Orbis Books, 1974); and Juan Luis Segundo, *Liberation of Theology*, trans. John Drury (Maryknoll, N.Y.: Orbis Books, 1976). For an introductory analysis of liberation theology, see Robert McAfee Brown, *Theology in a New Key: Responding to Liberation Themes* (Philadelphia: Westminster, 1978).

[25]As Arthur Cushman McGiffert argued in the conclusion of his *Protestant Thought Before Kant* (New York: Harper & Brothers, 1961), pp. 252–53, modern Rationalism, increasingly influential in shaping Western societies, remained anchored in the late-eighteenth century to the underlying principles of critical thinking and scientifically credible interpretations of events. This movement, in its various expressions, seemed to stand antagonistically opposed to the world and life view undergirding traditional Christian thought. Many thoughtful opinion leaders, though preferring a way for past and present mindsets to overlap or at least peacefully coexist, felt forced instead into a dilemma—either medieval and Christian or modern and agnostic.

[26]Friedrich Schleiermacher, *The Selected Sermons of Schleiermacher*, trans. Mary F. Wilson (New York: Funk & Wagnalls, n.d.); Pierre Teilhard de Chardin, *The Divine Milieu* (New York: Harper & Row, 1960); and Harry Emerson Fosdick, *The Meaning of Prayer* (Nashville: Abingdon, 1980).

[27]Robert M. Grant, *Gnosticism and Early Christianity*, rev. ed. (New York: Harper & Row, Publishers, 1966).

[28]Cyprian, *The Lapsed* and *The Unity of the Catholic Church*, trans. Maurice Bévenot (Westminster, Md.: Newman Press, 1957); Gregory the Great, *The Book of Pastoral Rule* and *Selected Epistles of Gregory the Great*, in Nicene and Post-Nicene Fathers, 2d ser., vols. 12–13, trans. James Barmby (Grand Rapids, Mich.: Eerdmans, 1956); Norman Cohn, *The Pursuit of the Millennium: Revolutionary Millenarians and Mystical Anarchists of the Middle Ages*, rev. ed. (New York: Oxford University Press, 1970); Martin Luther, *Table Talk*, ed. and trans. Theodore G. Tappert (Philadelphia: Fortress, 1967); Leland H. Carlson, ed., *The Writings of John Greenwood and Henry Barrow, 1591–1593* (London: Allen & Unwin, 1970); and Albert Peel and Leland H. Carlson, eds., *The Writings of Robert Harrison and Robert Browne* (London: Allen & Unwin, 1953). For an introduction to current representatives, see Millard J. Erickson, *Contemporary Options in Eschatology: A Study of the Millennium* (Grand Rapids, Mich.: Baker, 1977).

[29]Immanuel Kant, *Religion Within the Limits of Reason Alone*, trans. Theodore M. Greene and Hoyt H. Hudson (New York: Harper & Row, 1960); G. W. F. Hegel, *The Philosophy of History*, trans. J. Sibree (New York: Dover Publications, 1956); Albrecht Ritschl, *A Critical History of the Christian Doctrine of Justification and Reconciliation*, trans. John S. Black (Edinburgh: Edmonston and Douglas, 1872); and Walter Rauschenbusch, *A Theology for the Social Gospel* (Nashville: Abingdon, 1978).

[30]Friedrich Schleiermacher, *The Christian Faith*, ed. H. R. Mackintosh and J. S. Stewart (Philadelphia: Fortress, 1976), and Adolf von Harnack, *What Is Christianity?* trans. Thomas Bailey Saunders (New York: Harper & Row, 1957).

[31]Albert Schweitzer, *The Quest of the Historical Jesus: A Critical Study of Its Progress from Reimarus to Wrede*, 3d ed., trans. W. Montgomery (London: Adam & Charles Black, 1954).

[32]Martin Kähler, *The So-called Historical Jesus and the Historic, Biblical Christ*, ed. and trans. Carl E. Braaten (Philadelphia: Fortress, 1964).

[33]Nicolas Berdyaev, *The Beginning and the End*, trans. R. M. French (New York: Harper & Row, 1952); Rudolf Bultmann, *Theology of the New Testament*, 2 vols., trans. Kendrick Grobel (New York: Charles Scribner's Sons, 1951 and 1955); and Paul Tillich, *Systematic Theology*, 3 vols. (Chicago: University of Chicago Press, 1951–63).

[34]Wolfhart Pannenberg, *Faith and Reality*, trans. John Maxwell (Philadelphia: Westminster, 1977), and Jürgen Moltmann, *Theology of Hope: On the Ground and the Implications of a Christian Eschatology*, trans. James W. Leitch (New York: Harper & Row, 1967).

[35]Joseph Stein, *Fiddler on the Roof*, Pocket Book ed. (New York: Simon & Schuster, 1971).

2 How Am I Going To Do This?

A NSWERING THIS QUESTION reminds me of a couple reported to have taken an African safari. One morning the husband awoke to find his wife missing. Rushing out of the tent, he heard his wife's voice. Following her voice, he finally found her frozen, fifteen feet in front of a glaring lion. "What are we going to do?" she yelled. He responded, "The lion got himself into this mess; he'll have to get himself out of it!"

As the story suggests, one's point of view shapes the interpretation of data. Without discussing how to conduct historical inquiry, one's acquired method is left unexamined and likely flawed. This chapter begins with a highlighting of some of the points of view brought to this study at various times in the history of Christianity. Such a survey should create a context for current proposals, demonstrate the time-boundness of methods for studying historical theology, stimulate thought about legitimate guidelines for this type of research, and foster much-needed modesty when making proposals to guide current study. Discussion of the aim, materials, and principles of interpretation for studying historical theology follows this orientation.

A Survey of Past Approaches

How would inquirers in other times have approached the task of studying historical theology? As a matter of fact, Christians have interpreted their history with a variety of points of view. Through the following survey of some of these approaches, imagine being in the place of these other students. How would the interpretation of past thought have been affected?

What points of view might have been brought in the mid-third century to the study of Christian thought? If limited to "street thinking," students would have assumed history to be about the games the gods and lesser spiritual beings play with human beings.[1] However, those privileged by a good education would likely have been exposed to some combination of the variety of ways to interpret history circulating in the Greek and Roman world. The works of several Greek and Roman historians,[2] by promoting a critical and factual accounting of the past, would have provided a well-established methodological alternative to the traditional religious approach. Beyond methodology, several "philosophies of history" were present. Platonists would have taught them the immediate value of searching through life experiences for meaning is limited because the realm of ultimate reality, which transcends the sensual world and therefore history, is found through introspection.[3] Aristotelians would have encouraged them to look more seriously at life experiences to discover this realm of ultimate reality.[4] Stoics would have assigned meaning to life experiences in light of an already determined course for history set by a universal Reason.[5] Epicureans would have taught them that meaningful history is really about how human beings search for some sense of meaning and happiness in life apart from the gods.[6] Representatives of Persian philosophy would have tried to convince them that, since a distinct separation exists between spiritual good and material evil, history is the story of the cosmic conflict between these realms of reality.[7]

In the midst of such viewpoints, Christian instruction, while likely mirroring some of this current thought, would have focused on the idea of God's activity in creation, in the history of Israel, in the person of Jesus of Nazareth, in the ongoing life of the church, and in the judgment to come. Thus, early students of Christian thought would likely have been made aware of some of the several approaches to history circulating among the churches. Clement of Rome represented those who mined the resources of the past for examples to verify current beliefs.[8] Irenaeus explained history analogically in terms of God's effort to reclaim his "children" who have fallen through immaturity into rebellion.[9] Cyprian interpreted history more negatively as the decay of a fallen world.[10] Justin Martyr and Clement of Alexandria exemplified those who pointed to

Jesus Christ as the culmination of God's activity among Jews and Greeks.[11] On the other hand, Origen viewed history as the occasion for spiritual purging in anticipation of reunion with God.[12] Influenced by such interpretations, students would have regarded Christian history as the continued presence and experience of the work of God in Christ. At the same time, they might likely have engaged in less historical, more allegorical treatments of texts regarded as divinely inspired.

Those studying the history of Christian thought in the mid-fourth century would likely have expanded their method to include at least two new factors that accompanied the Emperor Constantine's rise to power with his victory outside Rome at the Milvian Bridge in 312. First, several church leaders followed Eusebius, bishop of Caesarea, in seeing the increasing social and political favor the church enjoyed under Constantine as an indication a new era in the redemptive economy of God had dawned.[13] The vision of a "Christendom" was born. Earlier conflicts between Christianity and the empire tended to be glossed over as tragic misunderstandings. Second, Constantine had introduced an innovative way to resolve recurring theological tension among Christians across the empire, i.e., an ecumenical or empire-wide council. While Christian leaders had met regionally for some time, they differed in their assessment of the place an ecumenical council headed by an emperor should have. Gradually, most church leaders came to regard such a council as making explicit the truth implicit in the apostolic witness and in this way maintaining continuity of thought within the church.

The sacking of Rome in 410 jolted the newly formed optimism about a Christian empire. How could such political and social disintegration be explained? Opponents of the Christian community seized the initiative by interpreting this as punishment from the gods for the favor shown the Christians. Orosius' *Seven Books of History Against the Pagans*[14] and Augustine's *City of God*[15] countered such opinions with a new Christian interpretation of history. Those studying the history of Christian thought in the late-fifth century likely would have utilized their point of view that history is the providentially designed story of the struggle between the city of God and the city of evil.

By the late-sixth century, cultural reversals and a political vacuum combined with recurring periods of plague and famine to create a popular certainty the world was coming to its end. Raised in a once glorious Rome wasted by the Gothic wars and Lombard invasions, Pope Gregory (d. 604) gave himself to the task of keeping the Western church afloat in those last days.[16] In the process, his other-worldliness affected historical research by questioning the value of earlier Greek and Roman historical interests to the degree they failed to contribute to preparation for the next life. Within this context, Gregory was instrumental in popularizing an Augustinian interpretation of history.

Though the end of history did not occur, the works of late patristic Christian historians continued to be normative for several generations.[17] Supplemented by biographies and chronicles,[18] they served well the Western church's commitment to what Vincent of Lerins spoke of as having been believed "everywhere, always, by all."[19] During the next several centuries, those studying the history of Christian thought would have followed the underlying method of memorizing and demonstrating the assumed continuity within the thought of the Fathers. However, as reflected in the twelfth-century writings of Anselm,[20] Abelard,[21] and Bernard,[22] this approach faced stiff challenges from the scholastic questioning method and the Aristotelian philosophy introduced in the newly emerging universities. Those studying historical theology at the late-thirteenth-century University of Paris, for instance, would have had at least two options from which to choose. If following the spirit of Bonaventure,[23] they would have adopted the more traditional approach which emphasized historical knowledge that verified or expanded other-worldly knowledge. If following the spirit of Aquinas,[24] they would have explored a more innovative approach which viewed human reason as reliable in gaining knowledge of this world and the result of such inquiry as worthwhile in its own right. Adherents to both these points of view would have remained loyal to the belief that a continuity of thought through the generations of Christian history held ancient and current theology together.

However, those studying Christian thought may have been reared at this time within one of the numerous sects that had arisen in opposition to the established church.[25] Here the thought of the church would likely have been interpreted as the story of the antichrist's success in leading the church into apostasy.

Subsequent to the time of Bonaventure and Aquinas, tension grew between those interested in the realm of nature and in the realm of grace. Promoting the former interests, universities[26] and creative writers[27] led Western societies into a new age. In such a setting, history as an academic discipline matured in an atmosphere less concerned about and often openly antagonistic to the more traditional religious approaches to the interpretation of history. The pre-Christian classical culture received renewed and at times uncritical examination. Embryonic textual criticism emerged. Unexamined recourse to miraculous interpretation of events waned. How might this have affected the study of Christian thought?

Humanistic education did not necessarily eclipse religious faith.[28] Nonetheless, the impact on Christian historical work varied. Some, following the lead of humanist scholars such as Erasmus, would have encouraged those studying Christian thought to recognize that church leaders through the centuries had differed significantly in their interpretations of theology.[29] Still, they would have maintained a conditional dependence on the history of Christian thought for explaining the Christian faith. However, others would have countered humanistic advances toward more objective historical method by urging students to employ a polemic handling of their past. Such a method produced interpretations of historical theology that supported already accepted views. For example, Matthias Flacius and other Lutheran scholars produced the *Centuries of Magdeburg* (1559–74). Cesare Baronius and other Catholic scholars responded with the *Ecclesiastical Annals* (1588–1607). Such efforts did call greater attention to and increase the availability of primary sources for historical research. Anabaptists[30] and English Separatists[31] tended to move even farther from improved historiography by interpreting the history of Christian thought so as categorically to dissociate themselves from what they regarded to be the church's complete departure from the path of God. By idealizing the beginnings of Christianity over against a subsequent apostasy, many among them, not surprisingly, marked in their time signs of the last days.

Those studying Christian thought between the Thirty Years' War (1618–48) and England's Great Rebellion (1640–60) on the one hand and the American and French revolutions on the other might have aligned themselves with a movement spreading across Europe which encouraged the effort to present Christian faith as essentially reasonable.[32] This orientation had definite implications for interpretation of Christian thought. Increased embarrassment about the medieval religious legacy of wars, intolerance, superstitions, and wranglings tended to encourage the reduction of historical probes to demonstrations of the juxtaposition of a "dark" past with an "enlightened" future. The history of Christian thought would have been measured by the thesis that essential Christian thought is reasonable, is compatible with common sense, and duplicates the natural religion now within the grasp of human reason. Some might have participated in the apologetic effort to present Christian faith as a republication of this natural religion.

By the late-eighteenth century, history's rise as a discipline with respectability in the university had converged with the then current tendency to limit the exercise of reason to empirical experimentation and verification. What did this scientific climate mean for the methods of historical research? First, greater objectivity became necessary. Some historians argued that eradicating personal involvement in the interpretation of history would free one to see the past more clearly. Second, a principle of analogy came to govern historical interpretation. By this principle, innovative historians attempted to interpret past events in light of scientific explanations of present events. In other words, they assumed themselves to be frequently in a better position to interpret past events than the participants themselves. Third, historians felt less and less restricted by the Christian idea of a chronologically short and providentially guided natural order. This made disciplines such as geology and archaeology increasingly important for interpreting the past.

Some believed they had found in this marriage of historical interpretation to modern methods of reasoning a medium to explain the meaning of human existence. G. W. F. Hegel argued that history is the combined and ultimately reconciled experience of the finite, human spirit and the Absolute Spirit.[33] Karl Marx countered that history has to do with the human struggle toward a social and economic structure that would free people to be truly human.[34] Arthur Schopenhauer reluctantly and pessimistically concluded that history had no meaning or aim.[35]

What did this more scientific approach to historical research mean for the study of Christian history? Though not without conflict, some Christian leaders believed this modern method for interpreting history could shed light on Christian history as well as provide a way to present Christian faith to modern societies. Thus, the late-eighteenth century ushered in a lengthy "quest" of the historical Jesus.[36] Historical criticism of Scripture flowered.[37] Adolf von Harnack, Reinhold Seeburg, and Alfred Loisy represent several scholars who pioneered reinterpretations of the history of Christian doctrine.[38] A late-nineteenth-century university student preparing for ministry, for instance, would likely have taken into historical studies this confidence in the convergence of an enlightened culture with the essential and now purged ancient faith.

Nevertheless, modern parallels to some of the worst traits of the spurned "dark ages" (e.g., an exploiting industrial economy and war) shattered, for many, confidence in enlightenment wisdom. Viewing the effort to find a historical ground for Christian faith as discredited, several young theologians sought to reestablish Christian faith on a foundation that proclaimed Christianity's existential intent and symbolic form.[39] The attention for studying historical theology in such an environment shifted to the rich resources in premodern historical records of religious experience, to a critical review of liberal theology, and to a proposed distinction between *Historie* (events subject to scientific historiography) and *Geschichte* (redemptive experience significant not only to past but future times and not necessarily subject to scientific historiography).

Since World War II, scholarly research into the details of the past has been increasingly accompanied by renewed interest in the broader interpretation of history's meaning. At least three factors account for this expanded agenda. Many have become frustrated with the immensity of apparently meaningless suffering and with social fragmentation that has reduced significant history to individual experience. Opinion leaders more readily acknowledge that the truth of science is not the whole truth. This recognition has encouraged a shift away from a closed world view that had rendered religious language senseless to a more open world view that admits the possibility of the unique. Couched in such cultural changes, several post-war Christian leaders have responded with a more historically rooted presentation of the Christian faith.[40] The extent to which historical methodology has been examined and altered has varied among these attempts to restate the relationship between history and theology.

Recommendations

As indicated by this survey, answers to the question, How should I do this? have varied. Still, while not claiming that any one answer is the final word on the subject, some answer must be given. The choice is between having an examined or an unexamined approach. Assuming desire for the former, think now about three starting points for answering the "how" question.

Aim

In historical studies, the end largely determines the means. When such study is a part of a curriculum, some aim merely to work off a required course. Others study Christian thought to prove themselves right rather than to pursue truth "as blind men long for light." Others aim to increase understanding, to learn, and to mature spiritually. The goal will govern the degree to which one will digest, reflect upon, and discuss new thought.

Those studying historical theology should look beyond merely "getting out by getting by" (if they are in a degree program) and beyond a polemic misuse of history to the more constructively critical aim of integrating this learning experience with devotional and ministerial formation. To this end, the following suggestions concerning materials and principles to guide the study are given.

Materials[41]

One can probe into historical theology only as far as the available tools allow. Ideally these tools include general reference works,[42] indices,[43] journals,[44] histories,[45] and series.[46] Such foundational resources, necessarily complemented by more specialized research, are commonly subdivided into primary and secondary categories. Primary material sheds immediate or direct light on the subject of the research. Secondary material sheds circumstantial or indirect light on the subject of the research. Primary material, in addition to formal publications, can come from correspondence, public records, art, prayers, speeches, and interviews. Secondary material includes contextual information, contemporary commentary, subsequent interpretations, and modern presuppositions. A source can be primary for subjects beyond the time and place initially addressed.[47] The same source can be either primary or secondary depending on the subject addressed.[48]

These basic resources make available the raw material for historical theology, i.e., the facts. Facts, which should be carefully distinguished from inferences about gaps in the facts available and from presuppositional judgments, are the fixed points for historical interpretation. Facts may be more or less significant to the subject being studied. Facts are never insignificant. Identifying "the facts of the matter," however, is not as simple as some might think.

First, access to facts is limited by the reliability of the sources to which appeal is made. Reference works should be used in a way that takes into account the biases of the compiler(s).[49] Primary writings at times suffer through translation.[50] Witnesses to proposed facts must be judged trustworthy.[51] Not all testimony stems from efforts to achieve historical accuracy.[52]

Second, access to facts is limited by the partial recovery of the facts. Even if all the facts could be gathered from all reliable sources, the historical sleuth would still be frustrated by the many facts that remain unknown.[53] Available facts can be overlooked.[54]

Third, access to facts is limited by the historian's proximity to the situation studied. Reducing the facts to those from personal or contemporary experience keeps the historian near current history, but distant from any history outside such narrowly drawn boundaries. If designed to expose students to a variety of cultures, education can shrink the ethnocentrism in historical judgments shaped by reference only to personal or contemporary experience. Journeying back through history by means of secondary resources can expand the historian's range of vision. Attention to the primary resources of past or present situations outside personal experience can greatly sharpen the historian's interpretations.

Locating and mastering the "nuts and bolts" of historical

theology is often tedious and less than exciting. Impatient students can easily become careless with the ongoing task of sifting out and remaining loyal to the data. Such students must be reminded that historical interpretations are only as dependable as their factual foundation. Still, the final significance of studying historical theology for Christian ministry lies in the interpretation of the available facts. For this, principles of interpretation are required.

Principles of Interpretation

One day on "Sesame Street," as he prepared to go to the library, Ernie heard the radio announcer mention a 50 percent chance of rain. Ernie's interpretation of this information led him to return for his umbrella, then his rain gear, then food for being stranded at the library, then a life preserver, and then his friend Burt. To interpret is to explain how the facts relate and what the facts mean. Ernie demonstrated what can happen when facts fall into the grip of unbridled imagination. Historiography, or the study of how historical research is conducted, has become a discipline in its own right.[55] This study has revealed that interpretations of history depend on several methodological principles, some of which may not be apparent to the interpreter. While rightfully humbled by this discovery, identifying influential principles can, nonetheless, contribute essentially to the reliability of historical research.

As discussed in chapter 1, certain principles of historical interpretation are inherent to the confession of Christian faith. For instance, history is believed to be fundamentally about the spiritual saga of humanity. History is seen as the stage for God's activity toward the realization of his will. History, therefore, is not viewed as beyond the possibility of events occurring that are unique to past experience. History, while cyclical to a degree, is regarded ultimately as a linear progression toward a divinely planned consummation. Modern historians, though, are distinguished by their use of foundational principles that call attention to the correlation of events, to the analogous relationship of present insight and past experience, to objectivity, and to ongoing self-criticism.[56] Can these spiritual and secular principles co-exist? The following discussion of modern principles of historical research is grounded in the premise that a Christian can be a responsible student of history and that a serious student of history can be a Christian.[57]

1. The Principle of Correlation has to do with the interconnectedness of events. Building on this principle, Christians studying history should regard historical research as more like watching a moving picture than viewing a collection of still shots. "The Meeting of the Minds" television series, with Steve Allen as master of ceremonies, illustrates this point well. Speculating on the discussion that would occur if Augustine (d. 430), Theodora (d. 548), Thomas Jefferson (d. 1826), and Bertrand Russell (d. 1970) were brought together is very stimulating and in many ways enlightening. The major drawback of such efforts is the absence of the context and personal development of the participants. The interconnectedness of events links the understanding of a specific historical subject to awareness of the ever-widening web of previous and subsequent experience.

Recognizing this dynamic character of history is not new. Heraclitus long ago noted that no one steps in the same river twice. For centuries, various forms of Platonic thought provided refuge from such apparent instability by pointing away from this life for a vision of what is really real. However, renaissance periods from the twelfth century forward have focused final attention more and more on this life with its changeableness. Physical sciences have accented the changing nature of the world in which we live. Social sciences have focused on the psychological and cultural dynamics of existence. Assertions of truth, to be taken seriously, must meet the test of giving meaning to changing life experiences. The impact of such thought has spread to other disciplines, including history.

What does this principle of the dynamic interconnectedness of events (correlation) mean for studying historical theology? Consider some examples. The use of this principle makes studying Jesus of Nazareth within his historical and cultural context necessary. Such factors as the Hellenistic impact on Palestine, current messianic and eschatological expectations, economic pressures, the state of theological formation, and his association with John the Baptist form a web of conditions that sheds light on Jesus of Nazareth. Or again, the use of this principle keeps the history of Christian thought from being chopped by centuries into independent time blocks. While transitions have occurred,[58] any one period in the history of Christian thought is understood to the degree that its antecedent web of events is known. Interpretation of the "high water mark" figures and moments in historical theology must reflect sensitivity to the story's interconnected and changing nature.

Students of Christian thought should check periodically their use of this principle (and the following ones). Historical thinking all too easily slips "out of bounds." On the one hand, they should ask if religious commitments have resulted in passing over or treating as insignificant the non-theological and yet historically observable questions and information making up the interconnected web. For instance, many generations of Christians, with comparatively little natural insight into the occurrence of events, have normally interpreted life experiences in terms of supernatural activity. The more recent recourse to natural regularities and randomness in explaining the occurrence of events has threatened this tradition. For historical research, students are out of bounds if they have met this potential threat by refusing to acknowledge the contextual web of history. God need not be eclipsed by thinking in terms of the interconnectedness of events. As several church historians have shown, non-theological factors do hold certain keys for unlocking the development in Christian thought.[59]

However, on the other hand, students of Christian thought should ask if their definition and use of the principle of correlation have led them to reject, even prior to investigation, the possibility that interconnected events may reflect personal intention and can, therefore, be distinct from previous experience. For example, some have felt compelled to choose between thinking scientifically and believing in prayers of petition. Harry Emerson Fosdick has offered one way out of the dilemma.[60] Fosdick argued that natural law and chance by themselves do not account for the existence of bridges, cars, houses, and the like. Personal planning and intention, working within current knowledge of nature, were involved. Reasoning from the lesser to the greater, Fosdick concluded that, once it is admitted human will can create events unique to past experience, the door is at least opened for taking seriously the idea that a superhuman will also can add to the web of events without violating previous interconnectedness. Today's ever-expanding microscopic and macroscopic knowledge of the world should keep students of history from claiming an exhaustive grasp of the story behind the interconnectedness of events.

2. The Principle of Analogy has to do with the privilege of interpretation held by historians who base their research on the insights of modern sciences in explaining present experience. According to this principle, if a correlation of events exists and if the sciences have sufficiently explained the present experience of such events, then the historian is justified in offering explanations of past events analogous to modern explanations of parallel events. Remaining differences are accounted for in a way consistent with the established similarities. This means that in a sense the modern historian may at times be in a better position to interpret the past than the actual participants.

This privilege of interpretation operates regularly when connect-the-dot puzzles are worked, when faces are "seen" in clouds, when a painting or plaque with a dot design suggests an object, when explanations of a car accident are offered by a passer-by who did not actually see the wreck occur. In each case, the observer sorts through previous experience to find an object or experience that makes sense of what is being observed. The principle of analogy operates in a similar manner in historical research.

Reasoning by analogy certainly impinges on the interpretation of historical theology. Take, for instance, the issue of demon possession. Common opinion into the eighteenth century backed the belief in literal demons indwelling human beings. However, as more and more people became disenchanted with such traditional beliefs, modern scientific advances seemed to offer them a natural alternative for explaining disturbed behavior. "Demon possession" has been modernized for many into a problem for psychology or psychiatry to resolve. Thus, when professionals today use medical diagnoses to unravel such phenomena as multiple personalities present in a single individual, radical mood swings, or bizarre behavior, historians feel safe in applying this analogically to the report of past conditions with similar symptoms.

Or again, take the issue of belief in the resurrection of Jesus. The use of the principle of analogy in historically analyzing belief in Jesus' resurrection has been a most serious challenge from modern historical methods for Christian apologists and theologians as well as Christian historians. Many believers and unbelievers have agreed that, since resurrection from the dead is not presently a part of observable experience, reasoning from analogy leaves the resurrection of Jesus as a proposed unique event beyond the historical verification possible for the crucifixion of Jesus.

In such cases, should the ideas of demonology and resurrection be rejected altogether? Should the resources of the sciences be rejected altogether? Can religious tradition and modern science be integrated? Such questions continue to undergird historical reflection on the Christian faith.

As with the principle of correlation, boundaries should also be observed for the definition and use of the principle of analogy. For a Christian doing historical research, this principle must undergird such efforts. Taking full advantage of modern insights into events, historical research should be built on the most reliable natural or human interpretations. This is referred to as "working from below." Students should periodically check to see if their Christian mindset has fostered a "fortress mentality" toward scientific or non-supernatural insights into events by which they either shut out all such resources from historical interpretation or predetermine that only modern insights which confirm traditional views will be considered. If so, their research is dangerously close to running aground.

For a student of history who is a Christian, the principle of analogy itself comes under review. Christian faith calls the student of history at least to take seriously interpretations unique to present understanding of experience. While beginning with natural explanations of the past, a Christian must refuse to demand that interpretations of the past reproduce current interpretations of present experience. Truth is not always and equally within the grasp of modern historiography. Those who are studying Christian thought should periodically check to see if their historical mindset has fostered a "fortress mentality" toward the possibility that the explanation best accounting for the data is an event unique to present experience.

The issue here is not the use of the principle of analogy but the assumptions accompanying its use. A Christian who intends to study history seriously seems to be in good position to take advantage of this principle.

3. The Principle of Objectivity calls for an overriding commitment to truth without personal distortions in historical research. As a young ministerial student, I witnessed a scene that abruptly forced me to think about objectivity. After listening to an admittedly unexpected speech, my father and I accidentally walked into the middle of a heated debate in the lobby. Pinned against the wall by several persons, the speaker was being verbally attacked. When the speaker finally had a chance to respond, he asked the person leading the attack, "Did you hear the speech?" He answered, "No, I did not hear the speech." His criticism had been based upon preconceived opinions and a short conversation with friends who may have left the auditorium even before the speech had been completed.

Should not the "golden rule" (Mt. 7:12) ensure that Christians will strive for objectivity in analyzing the thought and action of others? Though the question seems rhetorical, Thomas Merton has correctly observed that too frequently people prefer personal vindication over finding truth.[61] One manifestation of this, which incidentally continues to have occasional parallels in more recent Christian historical research, is the practice of uncritically and unconditionally superimposing a mold or model on historical data.[62] Sometimes this fallacy can produce quite unrealistic interpretations of the data.

One night my wife, then an eighth grade "straight A" student, was struggling with a thought problem in her algebra assignment. Though repeatedly applying what she was certain to be the correct formula, she could not come up with the answer in the back of the book. Very frustrated, she took the problem and her answer to her father, who, though a banker, had never studied algebra. She complained, "I know I have worked the formula right, but the book gives a different answer!" After quickly looking over her work, Bob concluded, "Jerrice, your answer *is* wrong." Now defensive, Jerrice responded, "How do you know?" To which Bob replied, "I've never seen a forty-two-ton cow before." Jerrice had so concentrated on a formula of x's and y's that she had failed to keep in mind the real life information in the thought question.

The models which have been imposed upon the data of historical theology, while not always producing forty-two-ton cows, have left interpretations somewhat short of objectivity. Those who have imposed upon the data the assumption of a continuity in Christian thought since apostolic days have tended to gloss over historically observable diversity of thought.[63] Those who have imposed upon the data the assumption of an early "golden age" of apostolic Christianity from which subsequent generations fell away have tended to overstate both the achievements of apostolic Christianity and the shortcomings of following generations.[64] Those who have imposed upon the data the assumption of the reasonableness of Christian faith have tended to mistake the limitedness of human wisdom for ignorant "darkness."[65] Those who have imposed upon the data the assumption that only conflicting thought preceded early Christianity's "orthodox" synthesis have tended to dismiss evidence of fixed points of identity among the first Christians prior to later formalization of thought.[66] Those who have imposed upon the data the assumption that history is essentially about economic class struggle have tended to deny anything more than a mirroring role for historical theology.[67] When any such archetype is treated as more important or authoritative than the available data, objectivity wanes.

In reaction to various ways historical interpretation had been apparently dominated by the interpreter's hidden agenda, several nineteenth-century historians followed the lead of Leopold von Ranke in arguing that historians could and must absolutely detach themselves from the subject being analyzed.[68] By late in the century, this aim was seen to have been unrealistic. Subjectivity crept into the thought of these historians, as well as other opinion leaders. They fell victim to their own criticism when their confidence in the results of enlightened inquiry softened their critical analysis of modern knowledge. Historians of Christian thought were not immune. Søren Kierkegaard, in his own time like a prophet crying out in the wilderness, argued that Hegelian rationalism had distorted interpretations of the Christian faith.[69] Albert Schweitzer, among others, argued that many historians in search of the historical Jesus, instead of describing Jesus of Nazareth, had in reality painted self-portraits in the name of Christ.[70]

Some, having surrendered the aim of objectivity, turned to impressionistic historiography in which self-portraits based on bits of data became common.[71] Others (with whom I sympathize), while admitting the impossibility of pure objectivity, have chosen more modestly to strive for the highest degree of objectivity.[72]

My father, in describing his role as a World War II navigator, has frequently commented on how much influence the weather had on his plane's reaching its destination. Among his responsibilities, he had to keep correcting the plane's course in order to approximate the intended time and place of arrival. Though his nickname was "pinpoint," he rarely had a "zero-zero" mission. When such precision accidentally occurred, he knew, as did all experienced navigators, not to report such because his peers would assume he had fudged the figures. Pilot error and instrument limitations made such precision luck.

Claims of objectivity in the study of Christian history are much like this. Be careful not to dismiss too quickly this biting reflection: "To historians is granted a talent that even the gods are denied—to alter what has already happened."[73] Since efforts to be objective in explaining the past will be laced with subtle subjective intrusions, those studying historical theology will need regularly to review how they have been framing questions, gathering data, analyzing data, using primary as well as secondary sources, and drawing conclusions. They should not be surprised to find themselves reflected in their research. At least some evidence of subjectivity can be detected in any one person's thought, particularly when reviewed by someone who approaches the subject from a different point of view. This reality supports the argument theologians as varying as Francis Schaeffer, Wolfhart Pannenberg, and John Cobb, Jr. have made for interdisciplinary discussion and writing.

Students of Christian thought should be alarmed, however, if they persist in forcing preconceived notions on the data. As forcing data into preconceived molds and models increases, illusions about history increase. On the other hand, if after their periodic review, such students still feel warranted in claiming "zero-zero" objectivity, they can be assured they have not looked closely enough. Harnack offered a bit of wisdom when, in his lectures on *What is Christianity?* he reminded his audience later generations would find "much hard and dry husk in what we took for the kernel."[74] He hoped for fair judges who would evaluate his generation on the basis of intent and improvement.

4. The Principle of Criticism requires recognition of the ongoingness of historical research. This means no effort to interpret history is beyond critical review and revision.[75] A healthy skepticism is believed to promote historical insight.

The type of reason promoted by Enlightenment leaders was critical reason. No sacred ground remained or could be claimed. Thus, modern historical criticism was born. When applied to Christian thought, those concerned about the apparent instability of historical judgments argued that truth common to all could not be dependent on "the accidents of history." For them, a mixture of philosophical and scientific reasoning took precedence. Others remained confident that critical reason would actually purge historical thought, thereby strengthening the contribution such knowledge could make. Anticipation that the real story would stand when the dust of historical criticism settled produced, among Christian historians, such monumental works as the multitude of "lives of Jesus," analytical surveys of church history and dogmas, and the collation and translation of many primary sources.

With the Enlightenment confidence having been broken by the late-nineteenth century, the principle of criticism came to be understood as implying a permanent relativity in historical interpretation. This development created a climate in which existential thinkers, opting more for subjective concern about personal meaning than objective interpretations of the meaning of the whole of history, could be taken seriously. Among Christians, historical attention shifted to form-critical interest in New Testament portraits of early Christians, to specialized historical monographs, and to identifying non-theological influences in the history of Christian thought. Since World War II, confidence that history has meaning and that this meaning can at least in part be detected has increased. Still, the principle of criticism continues to be recognized as fundamental to historical research. Perhaps this is most obviously symbolized by the practice of beginning publication titles with the indefinite "A" rather than the definite "The." Historical research and understanding entail an ongoing pilgrimage.

Efforts to approach historical theology with the principle of criticism can stray. On the one hand, those studying the history of Christian thought should check periodically to see if they have tended to be so dogmatic about their historical judgments that the principle of criticism has been discarded or minimized. Reasons to avoid this seem obvious. Subjectivity in research and reflections cannot be completely eliminated. Identification with the past situations is partial at best. Sources are limited.

At the same time, recognizing that historical judgments are based on partial access to the relevant evidence need not of necessity imply that any one judgment is as good as another. To illustrate, a photograph is a true but not exhaustive record of reality. My wife and I have an 8 x 10 photograph of our twin girls at ten months. While Erin did sit in a chair and Kimberly did stand by her side, the photograph did not capture the larger reality of a nervous father and grandmother crouched just outside the range of the camera in case the girls took a tumble. Similarly, historical interpretations can be true even though not exhaustive. they present the *ideal*, which captures the essence of the *actual* (see Fig. 2–1).

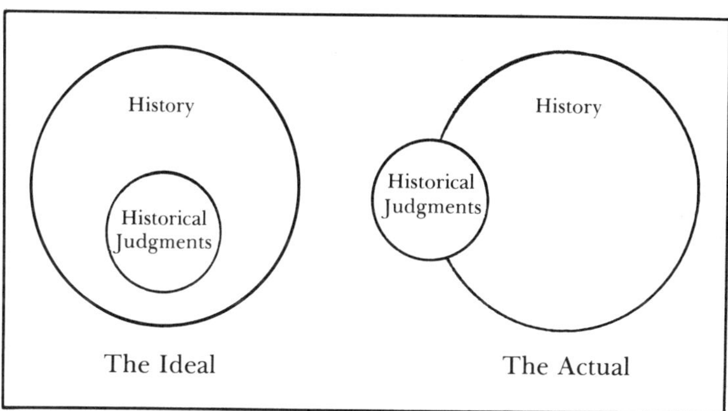

FIGURE 2–1

Since evidence exists only for what really happened, the principle of criticism promotes a clarifying of interpretations of this evidence. Subjecting historical interpretations to critical examination will help students approximate the aim to be accurate in their conclusions as far as they go.

Conclusion

Edward R. Murrow, legendary World War II correspondent and CBS radio/TV newsman, narrated a set of phonograph albums on which recordings had been made of such memorable events as Franklin Roosevelt reassuring Americans all they had to fear was fear itself; Neville Chamberlain naively announcing negotiations with Hitler had established peace; Winston Churchill offering a beseiged England blood, sweat, and tears; General Eisenhower encouraging his troops before the D-Day invasion; and Arthur Godfrey breaking down in his description of President Roosevelt's funeral procession. Murrow introduced such moments with the same line: "I can hear it now." Just so, the ultimate test of any method for studying the history of Christian thought is whether or not the living echoes from the past are heard in the present. Since those who are to be addressed by the past are also responsible for enabling the past to be heard in the present, the need carefully to examine how to study the history of Christian thought becomes obvious. Otherwise, those in the present unsuspectingly are left to hear only echoes of themselves.

Europeans joke about American tourists who claim to have "done France" or "done Italy" in one day. Similarly, this brief chapter has probed into many historical and methodological areas. As the notes indicate, many more detailed treatments are available to those whose curiosity or sense of urgency about methodology has been raised. However, others might prefer at this point, without spinning their wheels, a more entertaining type of reading. Such alternatives exist! Following the advice of my first college history teacher, I suggest that the habit of reading Sir Arthur Conan Doyle's tales of Sherlock Homes or Agatha Christie's mysteries be formed. Developing the ability to identify facts and to reason deductively about those facts can be fun.

Further Discussion

1. Try to recall your last history course. What were the aims and principles undergirding the course?

2. Why is the question, How am I going to do this? significant?

3. What are your aims for historical studies?

4. Why should Christian history not be divided into centuries?

5. What is the difference between dividing Christian history into centuries and recognizing that transitions have occurred in this history?

6. Evaluate Fosdick's proposal for dealing with the tension between faith and reason.

7. What are your criteria for determining the reliability of a witness?

8. Do you agree that a modern historian may have a "privilege of interpretation"?

9. What prejudgments are you bringing to historical research?

10. Is historical causation necessarily in conflict with supernaturalism?

NOTES

[1]Eli Edward Burriss, *Taboo, Magic, Spirits: A Study of Primitive Elements in Roman Religion* (New York: Macmillan Co., 1931); Mary Johnston, *Roman Life* (Chicago: Scott, Foresman and Co., 1957); and Harold Mattingly, *The Man in the Roman Street* (New York: W. W. Norton & Co., 1966).

[2]For Greek representatives, see Herodotus, *The Histories*, 4 vols., rev. ed., trans. A. D. Godley (Cambridge: Harvard University Press, 1946–50); Thucydides, *History of the Peloponnesian War*, 4 vols., trans. C. Forster Smith (Cambridge: Harvard University Press, 1951–53); and Polybius, *The Histories*, 6 vols., trans. W. R. Paton (Cambridge: Harvard University Press, 1954). For Roman representatives, see Sallust, *The Histories*, rev. ed., trans. J. C. Rolfe (Cambridge: Harvard University Press, 1960); Tacitus, *The Histories* and *The Annals*, 4 vols., trans. Clifford H. Moore and John Jackson (Cambridge: Harvard University Press, 1951–56); and Suetonius, *Lives of the Caesars*, rev. ed., trans. J. C. Rolfe (Cambridge: Harvard University Press, 1950–51).

[3]For introduction to and analysis of these points of view, see Edith Hamilton, *The Greek Way*, Norton Library Edition (New York: W. W. Norton & Co., 1964); Frederick Copleston, *A History of Philosophy*, vol. 1, pts. 1 and 2: *Greece and Rome*, Image Books Edition, 8 vols. (Garden City, N.Y.: Doubleday & Co., 1962); and appropriate articles in *The Encyc-

lopedia of Philosophy, 4 vols., ed. Paul Edwards (New York: Macmillan Co., 1967). Concerning Platonic thought particularly, see Plato, *The Republic*, trans. B. Jowett (New York: Random House, n.d.), and John M. Dillon, *The Middle Platonists: 80 B.C. to A.D. 220* (Ithaca, N.Y.: Cornell University Press, 1977).

[4]Aristotle, *Aristotle's Metaphysics*, trans. Hippocrates G. Apostle (Grinnell, Iowa: Peripatetic Press, 1979).

[5]J. M. Rist, *Stoic Philosophy* (London: Cambridge University Press, 1969); Seneca, *Letters from a Stoic*, ed. and trans. Robin Campbell (New York: Penguin Books, 1969); and Marcus Aurelius, *Meditations*, trans. Maxwell Staniforth (New York: Penguin Books, 1964).

[6]J. M. Rist, *Epicurus: An Introduction* (Cambridge: Cambridge University Press, 1972), and Epicurus, *Letters, Principal Doctrines, and Vatican Sayings*, trans. Russel M. Geer (New York: Bobbs-Merrill Co., 1964).

[7]Franz Cumont, *The Oriental Religions in Roman Paganism*, translation of the 1911 French original edition (New York: Dover Publications, 1956).

[8]Clement of Rome, "The First Epistle of Clement to the Corinthians," in *Early Christian Writings*, trans. Maxwell Staniforth (New York: Penguin Books, 1968), pp. 23–59.

[9]Irenaeus, *Proof of the Apostolic Preaching*, trans. Joseph P. Smith (New York: Newman Press, 1952).

[10]Cyprian, *The Lapsed* and *The Unity of the Catholic Church*, trans. Maurice Bévenot (New York: Newman Press, 1956).

[11]Justin Martyr, *The First Apology; The Second Apology; Dialogue with Trypho; Exhortation to the Greeks; Discourse to the Greeks; The Monarchy or Rule of God*, trans. Thomas B. Falls (New York: Christian Heritage, 1949), and Clement of Alexandria, *The Stromata*, Ante-Nicene Fathers, vol. 2 (Grand Rapids, Mich.: Eerdmans, 1975).

[12]Origen, *On First Principles*, trans. G. W. Butterworth (Gloucester, Mass.: Peter Smith, 1973).

[13]Eusebius, *The Ecclesiastical History*, trans. Kirsopp Lake (Cambridge: Harvard University Press, 1953), and *The Life of Constantine*, rev. and trans. Ernest Cushing Richardson, Nicene and Post-Nicene Fathers, 2d ser., vol. 1 (Grand Rapids, Mich.: Eerdmans, 1952).

[14]Orosius, *The Seven Books of History Against the Pagans*, trans. Roy J. Deferrari (Washington: Catholic University of America Press, 1964).

[15]Augustine, *The City of God Against the Pagans*, trans. George E. McCracken (Cambridge: Harvard University Press, 1957–72). For a secondary analysis of Orosius and Augustine, see Theodor E. Mommsen, *Medieval and Renaissance Studies*, ed. Eugene F. Rice, Jr. (Ithaca, N.Y.: Cornell University Press, 1959).

[16]Jeffrey Richards, *Consul of God: The Life and Times of Gregory the Great* (Boston: Routledge & Kegan Paul, 1980).

[17]For *The Ecclesiastical Histories* of Socrates, Sozomen, and Theodoret, see Nicene and Post-Nicene Fathers, 2d ser., vols. 2 and 3 (Grand Rapids, Mich.: Eerdmans, 1952). For an analysis of these his-

torians, see Glenn F. Chesnut, *The First Christian Histories* (Paris: Editions Beauchesne, 1977).

[18]Gregory of Tours, *The History of the Franks*, trans. Lewis Thorpe (New York: Penguin Books, 1974), and Bede, *A History of the English Church and People*, rev. ed., trans. Leo Sherley-Price (New York: Penguin Books, 1968).

[19]Vincent of Lerins, *Commonitories*, Fathers of the Church, vol. 7, trans. Rudolph E. Morris (New York: Fathers of the Church, 1949).

[20]Anselm of Canterbury, *Why God Became Man* and *The Virgin Conception and Original Sin*, trans. Joseph M. Colleran (Albany, N.Y.: Magi Books, 1969).

[21]Abelard, *Sic et Non*, as discussed by J. G. Sikes, *Peter Abailard* (New York: Russell & Russell, 1965), and Leif Grane, *Peter Abelard: Philosophy and Christianity in the Middle Ages*, trans. Frederick and Christine Crowley (New York: Harcourt, Brace & World, 1970).

[22]Bernard of Clairvaux, *Letters*, trans. Bruno Scott James (Chicago: H. Regnery, 1953), and *The Steps of Humility*, trans. George Bosworth Burch (Cambridge: Harvard University Press, 1940). See also, A. Victor Murray, *Abelard and St. Bernard: A Study in Twelfth Century "Modernism"* (New York: Barnes & Noble, 1967).

[23]Bonaventure, *The Mind's Road to God*, trans. George Boas (New York: Liberal Arts Press, 1953).

[24]Thomas Aquinas, *Summa Theologiae*, trans. Thomas Gilby, Timothy McDermott, Herbert McCabe, et al. (New York: McGraw-Hill, 1964–81). See also, Robert W. Shahan and Francis J. Kovach, eds., *Bonaventure and Aquinas: Enduring Philosophers* (Norman: University of Oklahoma Press, 1976), and David Tracy, ed., *Celebrating the Medieval Heritage: A Colloquy on the Thought of Aquinas and Bonaventure* (Chicago: University of Chicago Press, 1978).

[25]For detailed studies of medieval sects, see Jeffrey Burton Russell, *Dissent and Reform in the Early Middle Ages* (Berkeley: University of California Press, 1965); Norman Cohn, *The Pursuit of the Millennium: Revolutionary Millenarians and Mystical Anarchists of the Middle Ages*, rev. ed. (New York: Oxford University Press, 1970); and Edward Peters, ed., *Heresy and Authority in Medieval Europe: Documents in Translation* (Philadelphia: University of Pennsylvania Press, 1980).

[26]Hastings Rashdall, *The Universities of Europe in the Middle Ages*, 3 vols., ed. F. M. Powicke and A. B. Emden (Oxford: Clarendon Press, 1936); Lowrie John Daly, *The Medieval University, 1200–1400* (New York: Sheed & Ward, 1961); and Charles Homer Haskins, *The Rise of Universities* (Ithaca, N.Y.: Cornell University Press, 1967).

[27]Donald J. Wilcox wove discussions of such representatives as Boccaccio, Dante, Petrarch, and Machiavelli into his *In Search of God and Self: Renaissance and Reformation Thought* (Boston: Houghten Mifflin Co., 1975).

[28]Ida Walz Blayney, *The Age of Luther: The Spirit of Renaissance-Humanism and the Reformation* (New York: Vantage Press, 1957); H.

A. Enno van Gelder, *The Two Reformations in the 16th Century: A Study of the Religious Aspects and Consequences of Renaissance and Humanism*, trans. Jan F. Finlay and Alison Hanham (The Hague: Martinus Nijhoff, 1961); Paul Oscar Kristeller, *Renaissance Thought: The Classic, Scholastic, and Humanist Strains*, rev. ed. (New York: Harper & Row, 1961); and Joseph Anthony Mazzeo, *Renaissance and Revolution: The Remaking of European Thought* (London: Secker & Warburg, 1967).

[29]Erasmus, *Concerning Free Will*, trans. and ed. E. Gordon Rupp and A. N. Marlow, Library of Christian Classics, vol. 17 (Philadelphia: Westminster, 1969), and Matthew Spinka, *Christian Thought from Erasmus to Berdyaev* (Englewood Cliffs, N.J.: Prentice-Hall, 1962).

[30]Claus-Peter Clasen, *Anabaptism: A Social History, 1525–1618* (Ithaca: Cornell University Press, 1972); Robert Friedmann, *The Theology of Anabaptism: An Interpretation* (Scottsdale, Pa.: Herald Press, 1973); and Marc Lienhard, ed., *The Origins and Characteristics of Anabaptism* (The Hague: Martinus Nijhoff, 1977).

[31]B. R. White, *The English Separatist Tradition: From the Marian Martyrs to the Pilgrim Fathers* (Oxford: Oxford University Press, 1971).

[32]Immanuel Kant, "What Is 'Enlightenment'?" in *On History*, ed. White Beck, trans. Lewis White Beck, Robert E. Anchor, and Emil L. Fackenheim (Indianapolis: Bobbs-Merrill, 1963); Nicholas Capaldi, ed., *The Enlightenment: The Proper Study of Man* (New York: Capricorn Books, 1968); Norman Hampson, *The Enlightenment: An Evaluation of Its Assumptions, Attitudes, and Values* (New York: Penguin Books, 1968); and Henry F. May, *The Enlightenment in America* (New York: Oxford University Press, 1976).

[33]G. W. F. Hegel, *The Phenomenology of Mind*, trans. J. B. Baillie (New York: Harper & Row, 1967).

[34]Frederic L. Bender, ed., *Karl Marx: The Essential Writings* (New York: Harper & Row, 1972).

[35]Arthur Schopenhauer, *Essays and Aphorisms*, trans. R. J. Hollingdale (Baltimore, Md.: Penguin Books, 1970).

[36]Albert Schweitzer, *The Quest of the Historical Jesus: A Critical Study of Its Progress from Reimarus to Wrede*, 3d ed., trans. W. Montgomery (London: Adam & Charles Black, 1954); Fred H. Klooster, *Quests for the Historical Jesus* (Grand Rapids, Mich.: Baker, 1977); and Harvey K. McArthur, ed., *In Search of the Historical Jesus* (New York: Charles Scribner's Sons, 1969).

[37]Robert Davidson and A. R. C. Leaney, *Biblical Criticism*, vol. 3 of *Pelican Guide to Modern Theology* (New York: Penguin Books, 1970); Stephen Neill, *The Interpretation of the New Testament, 1861–1961* (London: Oxford University Press, 1964); Edgar Krentz, *The Historical-Critical Method* (Philadelphia: Fortress, 1975); Hans Dieter Betz, ed., *The Bible as a Document of the University* (Chico, Calif.: Scholars Press, 1981); and Richard N. Soulen, *Handbook of Biblical Criticism*, rev. ed. (Atlanta: John Knox, 1981).

[38]Adolf von Harnack, *History of Dogma*, 7 vols., trans. Neil Buanan (New York: Russell & Russell, 1958); Reinhold Seeburg, *The

History of Doctrines, trans. Charles E. Hay (Grand Rapids, Mich.: Baker, 1977); and Alfred Firmin Loisy, *The Birth of the Christian Religion* and *The Origins of the New Testament* trans. L. P. Jacks (New Hyde Park, N.Y.: University Books, 1962).

[39]Representing this generation of theologians in continental Europe were Karl Barth, Friedrich Gogarten, Edward Thurneysen, Georg Merz, Rudolf Bultmann, and Emil Brunner. The journal *Zwischen den Zeiten (Between the Times)*, which they established in 1922, broadcast for a decade their seminal ideas.

[40]Ernst Käsemann, "The Problem of the Historical Jesus," in *Essays on New Testament Themes*, trans. W. J. Montague (Naperville, Ill.: A. R. Allenson, 1964); Günther Bornkamm, *Jesus of Nazareth*, trans. Irene and Fraser McLuskey (New York: Harper & Row, 1975); Ernst Fuchs, *Studies of the Historical Jesus*, trans. Andrew Scobie (Naperville, Ill.: A. R. Allenson, 1964); Gerhard Ebeling, *Theology and Proclamation: Dialogue with Bultmann*, trans. John Riches (Philadelphia: Fortress, 1966); James M. Robinson, *A New Quest of the Historical Jesus* (London: SCM Press, 1959); Hans Conzelmann, *Jesus*, ed. John Reumann, trans. J. Raymond Lord (Philadelphia: Fortress, 1973); Leander E. Keck, *A Future for the Historical Jesus: The Place of Jesus in Preaching and Theology* (Nashville: Abingdon, 1971); Wolfhart Pannenberg, "Redemptive Event and History," in *Essays on Old Testament Hermeneutics*, ed. Claus Westermann and James Luther Mays, trans. Shirley Guthrie (Richmond, Va.: John Knox, 1963); and Pannenberg, *Jesus—God and Man*, 2d ed., trans. Lewis L. Wilkins and Duane A. Priebe (Philadelphia: Westminster, 1977).

[41]Norman F. Cantor and Richard I. Schneider, *How to Study History* (New York: Thomas Y. Crowell Co., 1967), and David Hackett Fischer, *Historians' Fallacies: Toward a Logic of Historical Thought*, Torchbook ed. (New York: Harper & Row, 1970).

[42]E.g., Henry Bettenson, ed., *Documents of the Christian Church*, 2d ed. (New York: Oxford University Press, 1975); G. Johannes Botterweck and Helmer Ringgren, eds., *Theological Dictionary of the Old Testament*, 4 vols., trans. John T. Willis, Geoffrey W. Bromiley, and David E. Green (Grand Rapids, Mich.: Eerdmans, 1974–); Jerald C. Brauer, ed., *The Westminster Dictionary of Church History* (Philadelphia: Westminster, 1971); Colin Brown, ed., *The New International Dictionary of New Testament Theology*, 3 vols., trans. G. H. Boobyer, Colin Brown, H. L. Ellison, et al. (Grand Rapids, Mich.: Zondervan, 1975); F. L. Cross and E. A. Livingstone, eds., *The Oxford Dictionary of the Christian Church*, 3d ed. (New York: Oxford University Press, 1974); J. D. Douglas, *The New International Dictionary of the Christian Church* (Grand Rapids, Mich.: Zondervan, 1979); Paul Edwards, ed., *Encyclopedia of Philosophy*, 4 vols. (New York: Macmillan Co., 1967); Marvin Halverson and Arthur A. Cohen, eds., *A Handbook of Christian Theology* (Nashville: Abingdon, 1958); James Hastings, ed., *Encyclopedia of Religion and Ethics*, 11 vols. (New York: Charles Scribner's Sons, 1955); Samuel Macauley Jackson, ed., *The New Schaff-Herzog Encyclopedia of Religious Knowledge*, 13 vols. (Grand Rapids, Mich.: Baker, 1949–57); B. J. Kidd, ed., *Documents Illustrative of the History of the*

Church, 3 vols. (New York: Macmillan Co., 1920–41); Gerhard Kittel and Gerhard Friedrich, eds., *Theological Dictionary of the New Testament*, 9 vols., trans. Geoffrey W. Bromiley (Grand Rapids, Mich.: Eerdmans, 1964–76); Dean G. Peerman and Martin E. Marty, eds., *A Handbook of Christian Theologians* (Nashville: Abingdon, 1965); Johannes Quasten, *Patrology*, 3 vols. (Westminster, Md.: Newman Press, 1962); and Philip Schaff, *The Creeds of Christendom*, 6th ed., rev. David S. Schaff (New York: Harper & Brothers, Publishers, 1931).

[43]E.g., *Biblia Patristica, Bibliography of Bioethics, Church History Index, Religion Index I, The Philosopher's Index, Religious and Theological Abstracts, Social Science and Humanities Index.*

[44]E.g., *Church History, Dialog, Interpretation, Journal of Ecclesiastical History, Journal of Ecumenical Studies, Past and Present, Second Century,* and *Theology Today.*

[45]E.g., Frederick Copelston, *A History of Philosophy*, 8 vols., rev. ed., Image Books (Garden City, N.Y.: Doubleday & Co., 1962); Hubert Cunliffe-Jones, ed., *A History of Christian Doctrine* (Edinburgh: T. & T. Clark, 1978); Will and Ariel Durant, *The Story of Civilization* 10 vols. (New York: Simon & Schuster, 1935–67); Justo L. Gonzalez, *A History of Christian Thought*, 3 vols. (Nashville: Abingdon, 1970–75); Adolf von Harnack, *The History of Dogma*, 7 vols., trans. Neil Buchanan (New York: Russell & Russell, 1958); Hubert Jedin and John Dolan, eds., *Handbook of Church History*, 10 vols. (vols. 1, 3–4, New York: Herder & Herder, 1965–70; vol. 2 and 5, New York: The Seabury Press, 1980; vols. 6–10, New York: Crossroads Publishing Co., 1981); Bob E. Patterson, ed., *Makers of the Modern Theological Mind* (Waco, Tex.: Word Books, Publishers, 1972–); and Jaroslav Pelikan, *The Christian Tradition: A History of the Development of Doctrine* (Chicago: University of Chicago Press, 1971–).

[46]E.g., *Ancient Christian Writers, Ante-Nicene Fathers, Fathers of the Church, Library of Christian Classics, Loeb Classical Library,* and *Nicene and Post-Nicene Fathers.*

[47]For instance, the writings of Aristotle, reintroduced in the West by the thirteenth century, are primary material for the study of medieval theology. The writings of Søren Kierkegaard are primary material for the study of post-World War I philosophy and theology.

[48]For instance, Irenaeus' *Against Heresies* is both a primary source for studying Irenaeus' thought and a secondary source for studying Gnosticism. Augustine's *Retractions*, written near the end of his life, is a secondary source for studying many of his earlier writings. Karl Barth's *Protestant Theology in the Nineteenth Century: Its Background and History* and *The Theology of Schleiermacher* are primary sources for studying Barth's thought and secondary sources for studying pre–World War I theology.

[49]Sometimes students quote encyclopedias and lexicons as the final word. However, to illustrate the flaw in this practice, take note that the fifteenth edition of the *Encyclopedia Britannica*, in an attempt to offer a systematic reading of the articles, includes a volume on "Or-

der of Knowledge" which reveals the editorial assumptions undergirding the series.

[50]This is demonstrated in the fate of Origen's *On First Principles* in the hands of his sympathetic Latin translator Rufinus. The 1973 Peter Smith publication of this work makes this clear by printing the Latin text and the original Greek fragments in parallel columns.

[51]The method used to determine if a potential witness is reliable has obvious significance for the results of the research. Intuition plays a part in deciding upon a potential witness's reliability. In order to test this "feeling," consider two checks. First, do not base the decision upon the potential witness's age, race, time of birth, infallibility, or agreement with present views. Second, in drawing a conclusion, do consider the potential witness's personal stability, motive, objectivity, openness, attitude toward others, personal commitments toward existence, authority, and impression on others interested in the testimony.

[52]Lorenzo Valla's exposure of the lack of historical reliability for the Donation of Constantine has come to symbolize the need for critical examination of texts. Form and redaction criticism have called attention to the other than historical interests behind the Gospels.

[53]Consider some examples from patristic theology. Several sources include speculation on the many years in the life of Jesus passed over in the Gospels. The letters of Ignatius briefly pull the curtains back from an early Christian leader whose life and thought are otherwise shrouded in mystery. The gap in information about Christian history between the apostles and the Apostolic Fathers is known as a "tunnel period." Several theories have been proposed to explain the origins of Gnosticism, evidence about which comes from the second century when Gnosticism was fully developed. Modern exchanges between Joachim Jeremias and Kurt Aland have demonstrated the cloud surrounding the early Christian roots of infant baptism.

[54]To illustrate, I saw *Fiddler on the Roof* many times before noticing that Tevye's third daughter, who was considered dead for marrying outside the faith, most literally fulfilled Tevye's Sabbath prayers for his daughters to be like Ruth and Esther. By analogy, a student of history must patiently sift through the materials time and again in search of the facts.

[55]In addition to the sources cited elsewhere in this chapter, see Mortimer Jerome Adler and Charles van Doren, *How to Read a Book: The Art of Getting a Liberal Education*, rev. ed. (New York: Simon & Schuster, 1972); Harry Elmer Barnes, *A History of Historical Writing*, 2d rev. ed. (New York: Dover Publications, 1963); Jacques Barzun and Henry F. Graff, *The Modern Researcher*, 3d ed. (New York: Harcourt, Brace & Jovanovich, 1977); Marc Bloch, *The Historian's Craft*, trans. Peter Putnam (New York: Alfred A. Knopf, 1953); Colin Brown, ed., *History, Criticism, and Faith: Four Exploratory Studies* (Downers Grove, Ill.: Inter-Varsity Press, 1976); John Cannon, ed., *The Historian at Work* (London: George Allen & Unwin, 1980); R. G.

Collingwood, *The Idea of History* (New York: Oxford University Press, 1956); Carl G. Gustavson, *A Preface to History* (New York: McGraw-Hill Book Co., 1955); C. T. McIntire, ed., *God, History, and Historians: An Anthology of Modern Christian Views of History* (New York: Oxford University Press, 1977); Hans Meyerhoff, ed., *The Philosophy of History in Our Time: An Anthology* (Garden City, N.Y.: Doubleday & Co., 1959); Allan Nevins, *The Gateway to History*, rev. ed. (Garden City, N.Y.: Doubleday & Co., 1962); Fritz Stern, ed., *The Varieties of History: From Voltaire to the Present*, rev. ed. (New York: World Publishing Co., 1976); and Arnold Toynbee, *An Historian's Approach to Religion* (New York: Oxford University Press, 1956).

[56]*Encyclopedia of Religion and Ethics*, 1955 ed., s.v. "Historiography," by Ernst Troeltsch.

[57]Van A. Harvey, *The Historian and the Believer: The Morality of Historical Knowledge and Christian Belief* (New York: Macmillan Co., 1966).

[58]E.g., from Jesus to the first Christians, from predominantly Jewish Christianity to a universal gospel, from illegal to politically favored status for the Christian church, from other-worldly to this-worldly interests, from pre–World War I optimism to post–World War I pessimism, and from predominantly Western European leadership in theology to indigenous theologies including "third world" nations.

[59]E.g., Adolf von Harnack, Jaroslav Pelikan, S. L. Greenslade, Martin Marty, Jean Daniélou, Hubert Jedin, John Dolan, and Justo Gonzalez.

[60]Harry Emerson Fosdick, *The Meaning of Prayer* (Nashville: Abingdon, 1980), pp. 87–107.

[61]Thomas Merton, *Conjectures of a Guilty Bystander* (Garden City, N.Y.: Doubleday & Co., 1968), p. 78.

[62]David Hackett Fischer, *Historians' Fallacies: Toward a Logic of Historical Thought*, Torchbook ed. (New York: Harper & Row, 1970), pp. 150–52, 216–42.

[63]Premodern scholars such as Peter Abelard, in his *Sic et Non*, and Erasmus, in his *Freedom of the Will*, were already calling attention to this fallacy.

[64]H. E. W. Turner, *The Pattern of Christian Truth: A Study in the Relations Between Orthodoxy and Heresy in the Early Church* (London: Mowbray, 1954).

[65]Blaise Pascal, *Pensees*, trans. A. J. Krailsheimer (New York: Penguin Books, 1966).

[66]Walter Bauer, *Orthodoxy and Heresy in Earliest Christianity*, ed. Robert A. Kraft and Gerhard Krodel, trans. Paul J. Achtemeier, Howard N. Bream, et al. (Philadelphia: Fortress, 1971).

[67]As illustrations, see the analyses of English Puritanism by Charles A. George, "Puritanism as History and Historiography," *Past and Present* 41 (December 1968): 77–104; and Christopher Hill, *Society and Puritanism in Pre–Revolutionary England* (New York: Schocken Books, 1964).

[68]Trygve R. Tholfsen, *Historical Thinking: An Introduction* (New York: Harper & Row, 1967), pp. 157–214.

[69]Søren Kierkegaard, *Concluding Unscientific Postscript*, trans. David F.

Swenson and Walter Lowrie (Princeton, N.J.: Princeton University Press, 1941).

[70]Albert Schweitzer, *The Quest of the Historical Jesus: A Critical Study of Its Progress from Reimarus to Wrede*, 3d ed., trans. W. Montgomery (London: Adam & Charles Black, 1954).

[71]David Hackett Fischer, *Historians' Fallacies*, pp. 103–30.

[72]Ibid., pp. xi–xxii.

[73]David Irving, *Hitler's War* (New York: Viking Press, 1977), p. xi.

[74]Adolf von Harnack, *What Is Christianity?* Torchbook ed. (New York: Harper & Row, 1957), pp. 54–56. Jasper Hopkins and Herbert Richardson, in their introduction to *Trinity, Incarnation and Redemption: Theological Treatises*, Torchbook ed. (New York: Harper & Row, 1970), p. xxii, found this to have been true of Anselm of Canterbury (d. 1109): "Where he is wrong, he is never foolishly wrong. If he could not escape the more problematical features of the intellectual milieu of his time, let it be said to his credit that he self-consciously worked to perfect that milieu rather than allowing himself to be quietly carried along by it."

[75]Examples confirming this methodological principle abound. Note the impact of the Dead Sea Scrolls discoveries on biblical studies, the Nag Hammadi discoveries on interpretations of Gnosticism, the reading of Søren Kierkegaard's *Journals* on interpretations of the works published during his lifetime, and the printing of Bonhoeffer's *Letters and Papers from Prison* on the interpretation of his *Cost of Discipleship*.

3 *How Do I Handle This?*

Thus far, this discussion has focused on crucial matters that arise before and during historical study. Now attention needs to be turned to the aftereffects of such study. Approaching historical studies as the previous chapters have suggested will produce certain questions not immediately germane to the historical task but definitely significant to devotional life and ministry.[1] One might doubt the value of study that does not have such implications for life.

One of the most frequent devotional concerns stirred by the study of historical theology has to do with attitudes toward the persons behind or represented by the thought being considered. Students are left to wonder, How should I view my own Christian heritage which has been shown to have both strengths and weaknesses? How should I regard people outside my religious heritage with whom the study of historical theology has acquainted me? Even though beginning from a variety of positions, those who enter a historical study of Christian thought find themselves drawn together as they better understand their differences and work their way toward a common theological center. As exposure to the history of Christian thought creates a more modest opinion about one's own thought and a more appreciative opinion about the thought of others, questions about the unity and division among confessors of Christian faith naturally arise.[2]

Robert Frost wrote of "The Road Not Taken."[3] He concluded that choosing the less traveled road had made the difference in his life. This chapter is devoted to an analysis of the roads more and less traveled by followers of Christ in dealing with unity and division among themselves. Undergirding this analysis is the conviction that the perspective brought to the handling of any specific situation where unity hangs in the balance makes all the difference.

Is Unity Important to God?

Few, if any, Christians would deny that unity is important to God. However, their behavior, if not their words, reveals that they differ greatly on how important unity must be to God. I believe that the God of Scripture is described as desiring and pursuing a vision of conciliation that should be manifest in how human beings relate to each other and their natural environment (Amos 1:9; Mic. 6:6–8; Mt. 22:36–40; John 17; 2 Cor. 5:17–21; Gal. 3:26–28; Eph. 2:11–22; 1 Jn. 1:1–3). Fundamental to the good news of the Christian faith is that God has continued to pursue these ideals even though spurned by an immature (at best) or rebellious (at worst) humanity. Still, God seeks to consummate the reconciliation formally established through the work of Jesus Christ. Thus, interpretations of the will of God should be centered on the ideals of conciliation, covenant, friendship, fellowship, love, peace, oneness, balance, harmony, and unity.

This being the case, the ministry of a church of the living God is the ministry of reconciliation. But can the message of reconciliation be taken seriously if not accompanied by a sacrificial pursuit of the reconciliation spoken of? What can be said of the roads more and less traveled by confessors of Christian faith when tested in reference to God's aim of reconciliation?

Exposure to the history of Christian thought presses students to examine the correlation of the message and the demonstration of reconciliation among followers of Christ. The conclusions frequently are not encouraging. In spite of good intentions, confessors of Christian faith through the centuries have generally worn down a path that has taken them far from their proclaimed and desired aim of reconciliation. Attention has repeatedly been called to Christians' silence about or open propagation of injustice, segregation, exploitation, and other conditions that contradict reconciliation. The easy availability of evidence supporting these charges makes denying such criticism futile. It is true: Finding followers of

Christ in the ranks of those striving for reconciliation has regularly been the exception rather than the rule.

Should this conclusion be disturbing? Ponder two demonstrations from Scripture of this matter's urgency. How did Old Testament prophets justify their alarming announcements that no knowledge of God could be found among the people? They did so by pointing to the injustice, exploitation, and violence that had resulted from the absence of a covenant of brotherhood (Isaiah 56–58; Jeremiah 9; Hosea 4–6; Amos 5–6; Micah 3). Or, why did Paul refuse to have Titus circumcised? Why did he publicly rebuke Peter, Barnabas, and others for withdrawing from association with Gentile Christians when visitors from Jerusalem arrived? He told his Galatian audience his actions had to do with preserving "the truth of the gospel" (Gal. 2:5) and being "straightforward about the truth of the gospel" (Gal. 2:14).

Is There Another Road for Christians to Travel?

1. Christ-centeredness

While studying the history of Christian thought adds many to the ranks of those who feel a sense of urgency about the fragmentation among confessors of Christian faith, too often persons awakened to the shortcomings of existing approaches have not clearly seen any alternatives. Consider then four signs of another road to travel which, though "less traveled by," promises to make "all the difference" in fulfilling the ministry of reconciliation.

The road that has repeatedly led confessors of Christian faith to experience a serious gap between the message and the demonstration of the reconciliation sought by God subtly shifts the traveler's point of focus off Jesus Christ when dealing with others. Without the mediation of Jesus Christ between them, these travelers are left to set themselves up as the standard for measuring others. Such comparisons spawn self-defense and self-promotion. Remember the childhood classic, "The Emperor's New Clothes"? Like almost everyone around the emperor, confessors of Christian faith have too frequently yielded to pressures to deny, minimize, or rationalize supposed deficiencies in their various religious heritages. Distorted impressions of others emerge. Fragmentation abounds.

As expressed by Figure 3–1–A, large blocks of people are viewed as outside the boundary and, therefore, the responsibilities of fellowship (Mt. 5:38–48; 25:31–46; Lk. 10:25–37). Even Jesus himself is forced to stand outside "the door" of such a group and knock for entrance (Rev. 3:14–22). Thus, the credibility of a message of reconciliation is undermined.

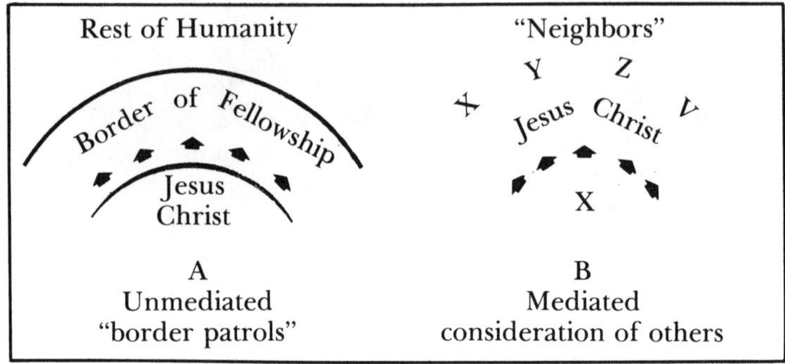

FIGURE 3–1

In traveling the road less frequently taken, disciples keep their eyes on Jesus (or, by analogy, continue thinking of Jesus) as they relate to others.[4] This primary focus on Jesus Christ as the mediator in all relationships keeps him in the position of the standard for measuring self and others (Mk. 9:38–41; Romans 14; 1 Cor. 12:12–26; Gal. 3:26–28; Phil. 2:5–11; and Heb. 12:1–2). Here fellowship with Jesus Christ creates and sustains a radical restructuring of the disciples' relations to others. Responsibility for acting upon a real sense of brotherhood with every human being and all of God's creation is restored. Reflecting a knowledge of the God revealed in Scripture and by Jesus Christ, disciples too become reconciled to the world (see Figure 3–1–B). Questions of fellowship among confessors of Christian faith, then, have to do with the degree or quality of the fellowship created and recreated by God in Christ (Philemon 15–17).

Maintaining the mediation of Jesus Christ when relating to others eliminates the habit of overstating the spiritual health of one's religious heritage. Noted politicians have on occasion explained the relation of their political views to what has been passed on to them by pointing to three possible ways of dealing with a diseased or damaged tree. They have noted that one can deny the tree has any problem, or chop the tree down at its base regardless of the state of the problem, or treat the tree so as to preserve the tree's strength and usefulness. Politicians generally opt for the last. Though perhaps not immediately apparent, what has been religiously passed on is best served by such a constructively critical approach that magnifies strengths and calls for the correction of mistakes. In this way, tradition can be meaningfully subordinated to and transformed by the light of truth. Christ-centeredness may lead to strained relations with or even dissociation from one's religious heritage. However, because of respect for those who have contributed to this heritage and because of existing relationships for ministry, this decision should be made with regret and only when denied the possibility of continuing to "seek first the kingdom of God" (Mt. 6:33).

Also, maintaining the mediation of Jesus Christ in forming impressions of others protects disciples from inaccurate and embarrassing prejudgments about others (Mt. 7:1–5). Imagine the existing impressions that preceded the recently converted Saul of Tarsus when Barnabas escorted him to Jerusalem. Imagine Philemon's view of Onesimus before he broke open the letter that accompanied the returned slave. The effectiveness of Barnabas and Paul in correcting these misconceptions depended on the willingness of those addressed to suspend judgment long enough to listen and learn. The same is true today. Viewing others in light of Jesus Christ creates the attitude necessary (Mt. 7:12) for stereotypes of others to be replaced by understanding.

Consider the following parable. A physical education teacher of seventh-grade boys announced that the highlight of the spring semester would be a hundred-yard race to be run on the first Saturday in May. The boys worked diligently in preparation for the race. The teacher watched the boys arrive with their proud parents at the football field on a beautiful May 3. As they approached the starting line, four boys caught his attention. Johnny had been the best runner all semester. Watching him warm up, the teacher knew he would cross the finish line first. Billy had weighed about 150 disproportioned pounds at the beginning of the semester. Though still a bit out of shape, he had shed fifteen pounds during the semester. His parents had commented to the teacher that they were so pleased Billy was no longer embarrassed about his appearance. Joey limped to the starting line. The teacher had heard about the boy from colleagues. Joey had been born with a deformed leg. However, his parents had faithfully worked with him. The teacher never saw Joey fail to complete an exercise run. Little Timothy and his parents wore most moving smiles. The teacher had been concerned about Timothy when the class started. He had been very distant, constantly coming up with excuses to get out of exercising and running. The teacher soon discovered Timothy had a respiratory problem. After assuring Timothy and his parents that any emergency could be handled, the teacher had gradually and carefully trained the boy. Standing one-hundred yards away, the teacher dropped the flag. The race began. As expected, Johnny crossed the finish line twenty yards ahead of the others. Billy struggled across the finish line thirty yards behind. Joey completed the hundred yards though far behind the rest. Timothy gave his all until he could not breathe well enough to continue. He completed sixty yards. Who left the field a winner?

Viewing self and others through the mediation of Jesus Christ, disciples are less likely to forget that God ultimately judges the participants in the race of life (e.g., Mt. 7:1–5; Mk. 9:38–41; Lk. 10:25–37, 18:9–14; Acts 10:1–23; Rom. 2:1–29; 14:1–15:13; Gal. 2:1–21; Jas. 2:1–13). Scripture repeatedly illustrates that God's judgments frequently counter human expectations (Jonah; Amos; Mt. 7:21–28; 25:31–46; and Romans 9–11). This should provide ample motivation for pursuing a road that enables confessors of Christian faith to recognize, not judge, "the servant of another" (Romans 14).

2. *Diversity*

The road that has repeatedly led confessors of Christian faith to experience a serious gap between the message and the demonstration of the reconciliation sought by God leaves its travelers little room for diversity (Mk. 9:38–41; Acts 15; Romans 14; Gal. 2:1–21; Jas. 2:1–13). Individuals or groups that set themselves up as the standard by which others are measured resist receiving critical self-examination, admitting inadequacies, considering alternatives, or initiating change. Instead, the need to be proved right eclipses an open longing for truth. What inquiry is allowed must confirm existing views and practices. Pressure to be clearly dissociated from others

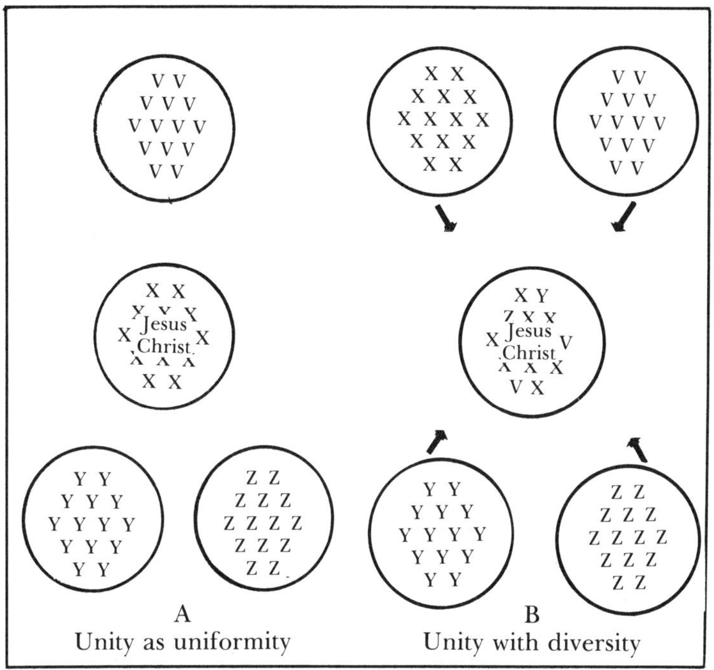

FIGURE 3–2

different from themselves restricts what is said and done in the name of Christ. With freedom smothered by equating unity with uniformity, is the oft-resulting economic, racial, cultural, and religious sameness among isolated groups of Christians surprising? The universal and reconciling intent of the gospel is hemmed in by attempts to minimize variation among followers of Christ (as expressed in Figure 3–2–A). Clay is taken from the potter's hand (Romans 9).

However, traveling the road less frequently taken involves an essentially positive attitude toward the role that variation plays in the demonstration of the reconciliation sought by God. Sameness is certainly acceptable when it happens to occur. Nevertheless, unity here has to do with interdependence, balance, harmony, mixture, and cooperation among the broad, diverse spectrum of people God intends to bring together as "one new man" (1 Cor. 12:12–26; Eph. 2:11–22). God in creation has surrounded human beings with many demonstrations that the divine conception of unity is not threatened by diversity. Recall the range of creatures identified as "dog," or "fish," or "human." The same is true of plants. Life is sustained by the interdependent differences between plants and animals. Also, families, communities, nations, faculties, athletic teams, orchestras, and the like magnify the same point. Diversity is contrary to uniformity, not to unity. In Christian faith, walls of division are torn down by putting on Christ. Human variations are baptized into Christ. Economic, social, racial, sexual, and religious terms which as nouns divide human beings become in Christ adjectives that describe human beings undergoing unique re-creation by God. This means that a church truly of Christ will be made up of an inclusive diversity of persons united in the overarching identity found in Jesus Christ (as illustrated by Figure 3–2–B). This basic identity shared by followers of Christ allows the radical adaptability to others (1 Cor. 9:22) necessary for demonstrating reconciliation and encourages the creative exercise of freedom in Christ necessary for spiritual growth.

3. Truth

The road that has repeatedly led confessors of Christian faith to experience a serious gap between the message and the demonstration of the reconciliation sought by God forces its travelers to separate the concept of unity from the concept of truth, restricting unity to a desirable by-product of truth (Figure 3–3–A). With unity thus set apart from consideration of truth, little centripetal force remains to keep followers of Christ from breaking away into a multiplicity of splinter groups. The resulting list of causes for division becomes almost endless. Initiating or continuing these divisions is defended as the result of "standing for the truth." An unfortunate complacency about fragmentation often develops. Much like the fish that become so convinced of the glass divider in the aquarium they continue to swim only on one side of the aquarium when the divider is removed, separated brethren in time get used to divisions.[5]

In traveling the road less frequently taken, disciples understand unity to be not only an experience but also an essential component of what truth is (see Figure 3–3–B).[6] Here truth is defined in personal terms of relationship (Hos. 4:1–6; Jn. 8:32; 14:6; 17). Certainly truth continues to be contrasted, as

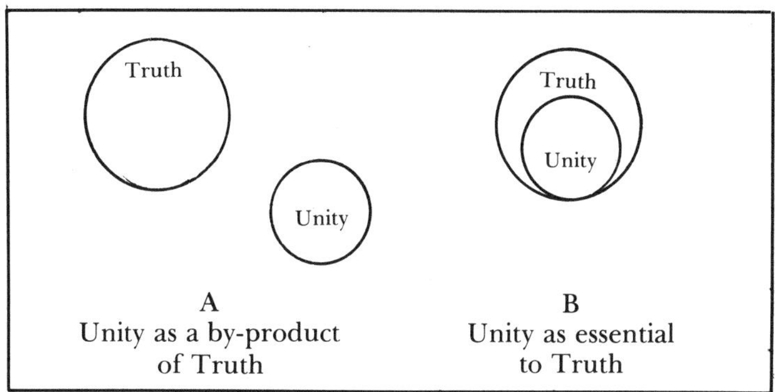

FIGURE 3–3

in a "true-false" test, with what is logically or empirically "false." Yet basically, truth is contrasted with illusory, deceptive, or distorted interpretations of reality. Does this conception of truth sound strange? If so, one reason is that Western cultures have not retained much of this more Eastern view of truth. Remember Christianity is rooted in the ancient Near Eastern context that surrounds the Bible.

But what does this have to do with unity? When "life under the sun" is indiscriminately observed with this view of truth, conflict and self-interest appear to describe accurately what is true or real about human experience. However, disciples traveling the road less frequently taken see such a conclusion as lacking the revelation of God in Jesus Christ about what is ultimately true or real. Truth as defined by God essentially, though not exclusively, has to do with unity. This explains God's persistent work against hostile or tolerated divisions that inhibit reconciliation among human beings. A "standing for truth" that initiates, accepts, or continues divisions is also a sacrifice of truth. Standing for unity is also standing for truth. With this view of the relation of truth and unity, reasons for a lack of fellowship among followers of Christ must be demonstrated to be more important to God than unity. Since truth has to do with more than unity, fragmentation may become necessary. Even so, concern for the realization of all truth, defined to include unity as an essential component, sustains a deep sense of urgency about such fragmentation. This urgency is manifest in repentance, in continued prayer, and in efforts to resolve existing broken relationships.

As these thoughts indicate, traveling this road less frequently taken establishes sacrificial ministry in the "marketplaces" of society (Mk. 6:54–56) as the proper location for theological and devotional reflection on the reconciliation actively sought by God. The importance of issues or problems is difficult to determine when considered in the easily sterile and impersonal environment of a classroom, a building, or a retreat (Matthew 23). However, in traveling this road less frequently taken, disciples have their consideration of Christian unity purged by being with and ministering to the people in need of the mending balm of God's reconciliation in their lives. How would discussions concerning truth and unity be affected if conducted in a bus depot, a university student center, a housing project, a children's hospital waiting room, an unemployment line, a refugee camp, a shopping mall, or a nursing home parking lot?

4. Change

The road that has led confessors of Christian faith to reflect a serious gap between the message and the demonstration of the reconciliation sought by God encourages its travelers to be suspicious of and to resist change (Figure 3–4–A). Recalling

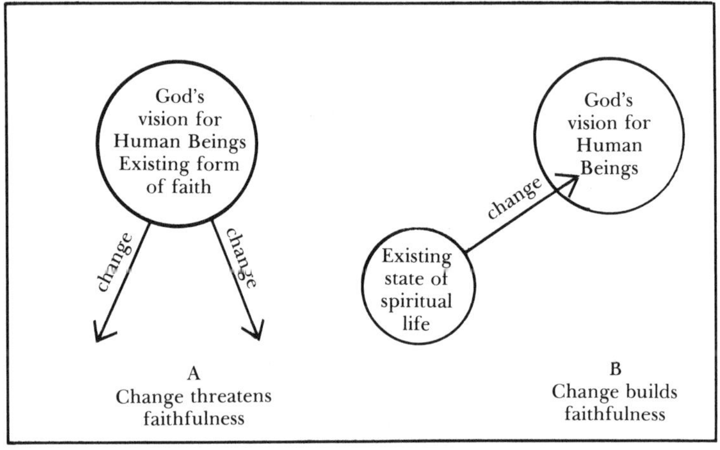

FIGURE 3–4

again the provocative play *Fiddler on the Roof*,[7] the fiddler accurately symbolizes the dynamics of existence. His position on the roof points to the precarious circumstances of life (Eccl. 9:11–12), in which one can quickly fall and "break his neck." His fiddling represents a person's humble expectation of "scratching out a pleasant tune" in life. Surrival depends on balance and a confidence about "who he is and what God expects him to do." Since the life situation in Anatevka had remained the same for "many, many years," this balance and identity had been maintained by the "Tradition" that had been passed from one generation to another with very little change. The play portrays a variety of reactions to the reshaping of this life situation caused by the inbreak of the "new," "outside" world.

Confessors of Christian faith, following the more traveled road, have tended to reflect the common satisfaction with "things as they are" and have been for "many, many years." While a pendulum swing to "change for the sake of change" has no warrant, being predisposed against change sacrifices loyalty to truth, freezes existing weaknesses, and distorts self-understanding. Such a posture does not foster the sense of urgency and the courage needed to allow God to "have his own way" in closing the gap between the message and the demonstration of reconciliation.

In traveling the road less taken, disciples accept change as integral to spiritual identity and balance for living. Boys seeking to qualify for second-class ranking in Boy Scouts have to complete a five-mile hike. Before embarking cross-country toward our chosen destination for my hike, my father and I took an initial reading from my compass. If we had used the compass only this one time or if I had insisted on using the compass without my father's aid, I have little doubt we would have completely missed our destination. Even with repeated course corrections, we ended a few hundred yards north of the mark.

In the same way, those following the less traveled road find security in the freedom and readiness to change. God has surrounded human beings with indications that natural life is sustained by change. Discussion in Scripture of the history of Israel and the first Christians, as well as such themes as repentance, discipleship, spiritual growth, teachableness, and resurrection prove that this is true for spiritual life as well.

Perhaps this trait of the less traveled road is the cornerstone to the prospects for followers of Christ to be drawn nearer to the reconciliation sought by God. The courage to change makes disciples receptive to the transforming impact of Jesus Christ (Figure 3–4–B). The courage to change enables followers of Christ to adapt to the indiscriminate, inclusive family God draws to himself. The courage to change frees confessors of Christian faith to act upon the results of seriously asking, "What is more important to God than unity?"

Conclusion

Late one night an American tourist, who had spent the day enjoying the Tower of Pisa, discovered he had boarded a train bound for Bologna, not Rome where his possessions and hotel were. His only choice—change trains. Such is the situation facing so many followers of Christ. No attempt has been made in this chapter to address directly any of the myriad of issues and problems that have strained or severed ties among confessors of Christian faith. Such an attempt is premature if commitment to the destination of reconciliation is subordinated to or made conditional upon the resolution of the specific issues and problems. Instead, the focus of this chapter has been on the attitudes and strategy that deeply influence how such specifics are dealt with. As with the tourist, the most basic decision facing many followers of Christ comes with the discovery that the road they are traveling is leading them away from their confessed destination and with the identification of a road that promises to lead them toward their intended destination. For Christians, the desired destination is not negotiable: to know God. But coming to know the God of Jesus Christ means coming to know the reconciliation God wills. With commitment to this destination established, the "roads" more and less traveled can then be described and evaluated. The ultimate decision is with destination more than route. Those who study the history of Christian thought are challenged to step away from the beaten path to follow a "road less traveled." This move is justifiable only as a natural result of being drawn nearer to God's vision of conciliation.

Further Discussion

1. Read Ezekiel and Jeremiah. Discuss their attitudes toward Israel and toward their tasks.

2. What do the letters to the seven churches in Asia (Revelation 2–3) suggest about attitudes toward one's religious heritage?

3. Critically evaluate the mediated and unmediated mindsets.

4. Can a person holding an unmediated outlook approach the study of historical theology as suggested in chapters two and three?

5. What do you understand to be the minimum necessary for Christian identity?

6. What do you think is more important to God than unity?

7. How would you explain the relationship of truth and unity?

8. What place does change have in your religious heritage?

9. Are there other devotional or ministerial questions stirred by studying historical theology?

NOTES

[1]Hubert Cunliffe-Jones, ed., *A History of Christian Doctrine* (Edinburgh: T. & T. Clark, 1978), pp. 11–20.

[2]For further reading on Christian unity, see A. M. Allchin, *The Living Presence of the Past: The Dynamic of the Christian Tradition* (New York: The Seabury Press, 1981); S. L. Greenslade, *Schism in the Early Church*, 2d ed. (London: SCM Press, 1964); Norman Goodall, *The Ecumenical Movement: What It is and What It Does*, 2d ed. (New York: Oxford University Press, 1964); Hans Küng, ed., *The Future of Ecumenism* (New York: Paulist Press, 1969); John T. McNeill, *Unitive Protestantism: The Ecumenical Spirit and Its Persistent Expression*, rev. ed. (Richmond, Va.: John Knox, 1964); E. L. Mascall, *The Recovery of Unity: A Theological Approcah* (New York: Longmans, Green & Co., 1958); and Ruth Rouse and Stephen Neill, eds., *A History of the Ecumenical Movement*, rev. ed. (Philadelphia: Westminster, 1967–70).

[3]Robert Frost, "The Road Not Taken," in *Robert Frost's Poems*, Pocket Book ed. (New York: Simon & Schuster, 1971), p. 223.

[4]Dietrich Bonhoeffer, *The Cost of Discipleship*, rev. ed., trans. R. H. Fuller and Irmgard Booth (New York: Macmillan Co., 1977).

[5]Jürgen Moltmann, *The Passion for Life: A Messianic Lifestyle*, trans. M. Douglas Meeks (Philadelphia: Fortress, 1978).

[6]Emil Brunner, *The Divine–Human Encounter*, trans. Amandus W. Loos (London: SCM Press, 1944).

[7]Joseph Stein, *Fiddler on the Roof*, Pocket Book ed. (New York: Simon & Schuster, 1971), pp. 3–10.

4 *When Am I Ready To Make Use of This?*

MOSES SPENT FORTY YEARS shepherding in the land of Midian before he was ready to lead the Israelites out of Egyptian slavery. Both Jesus and John the Baptist were around thirty before becoming very visible as religious servants. The counsel sent to Timothy repeatedly warned against religious neophytes being placed in leadership roles. The servants of God mentioned in Scripture are almost without exception persons seasoned by life and by meditation. Can this be dismissed as coincidence? Or is there some lesson about readiness for ministry to be gleaned from these stories? The fundamental thesis of this volume is that exposure to the history of Christian thought can make significant contributions to Christian growth and ministry. Faith can be refreshed. Self-examination can be deepened. Fellowship can be broadened. The study of Scripture can be enriched. Theological reflection can be brought into balance. Nonetheless, these contributions are not guaranteed; spiritual maturity will ultimately make the difference.

Readiness for a task is difficult to determine prior to actual experience in the situations for which persons prepare. Some combination of age limits, prior behavior, formal training, and skill development are used in assessing readiness to marry, to vote, to drive, to serve in the military, to hold public office, to teach, to practice medicine, and to practice law. Frequently, readiness for Christian ministry has been judged by this same cluster of factors. The rationale for this measurement of readiness for social or religious responsibilities is that, though not guaranteeing the person's qualification, these factors are trusted to weed out unprepared applicants.

However, what do these external and somewhat arbitrary factors actually reveal about the maturity necessary for Christian ministry? Passing these tests does not guarantee readiness. Failing these tests does not eliminate readiness. Among the exemplary servants of God remembered in Scripture, some were ridiculed because of their youth, some had questionable pasts, some possessed limited skill, and most lacked formal training.

Readiness for Christian ministry is tied to a person's acquiring the mind of Christ (Mt. 16:24–26; 1 Pet. 2:18–25; Rom. 8:12–30; 12:1–2, Gal. 4:19; Phil. 2:1–11; John 6; 1 John 5). Some who study the history of Christian thought can become more historically informed than devotionally reformed or conformed.[1] This gap must be closed before the study of historical theology becomes useful for service in the name of Christ. The following discussion is an attempt to identify signs both of immaturity and of the passage into the maturity necessary for Christian service.

Theological Adolescence

Helmut Thielicke has described the identity crisis ministerial students experience in their academic training as theological puberty.[2] The illustration is very effective. The mention of "puberty" resurrects an assortment of teenage memories. Puberty brings such biological changes as stumbling because of sudden spurts of growth, embarrassing voice breaks, sexual awakening, and nagging complexion problems. These biological manifestations of puberty are compounded by unpredictable moodiness, incorrigibility, and hidden fears of adulthood. These traumatic experiences can be humorously remembered when the passage through adolescence is past. However, adolescence itself is not so humorous. Teenagers, being neither children nor adults, are confused about their identity. Adults maintain patience with teenagers as they struggle toward maturity in part because of their potential for shouldering future responsibilities.

Puberty is a rich analogy for describing the theological and devotional experience of more than a few who study historical theology. Since this problem tends to be most acute for college and graduate students of religion, their experience exemplifies the struggle also present in less severity for others. Formal training throws these students into an elite status among confessors of Christ. After all, how many others can read Hebrew or Greek? How many know of the backgrounds to Scripture? How many know enough of Christian history to trace the roots of their thought and practice? How many are acquainted with the questions and alternatives of scholarship? These students initially handle their elitism in predictably adolescent ways. Language that simplifies scholastic discussions becomes fog to their attempts to speak with "common" folk before whom they indiscriminately parade specialist vocabulary. They find ways to display their new skills. They are primarily concerned about their performance in public speaking. They tend either rarely to admit "I don't know" or humbly to recite their questions about every subject. They regularly snipe at the "uninformed" in group discussions. Disregarding the warning in "Oh, that mine adversary had written a book," they rush to get their opinions "on the record." They trample down tradition.

This problem of theological puberty is compounded by the fact that these students are frequently unaware of their condition. Sometimes among raw recruits in bootcamp, some soldiers have to wear red helmets. These are the Gomer Pyles whose guns somehow fired live ammunition after three gun checks at the firing range, whose grenades landed only a few feet beyond the protective barrier, who forgot their sextant on practice flights, and who hit the plane pulling the target during gunner practice. The red helmets signal their danger to others. While students in the throes of theological puberty are not marked off in so tangible a way as a red helmet, those around them have little trouble detecting their presence.

Each department in a theological curriculum produces particular manifestations of theological puberty. Historical theology is no exception. For instance, adolescence among students of historical theology is evident in their frequent "eye to eye" approaches to those to whom they are being introduced. With little "frontline" experience and with partially acquired skills, they claim quickly to see through an Augustine, a Calvin, a Barth, or a Bultmann.

When speaking with persons not acquainted with historical theology, adolescent students find it difficult to resist the temptation to drop hints of their knowledge. Those listening rightfully wonder, as did a young boy who heard a preacher talk twenty minutes about his foreign travel, What was that about? Just as the boy's father saw that "the preacher wanted us to know he has been to South America," so also those listening to adolescent recitation of historical theology material realize that "he wants us to see what he knows." By this display of what they do know about historical theology, adolescent students inevitably have their image puffed up, like cotton candy, into "expert." After all, what *Fiddler on the Roof's* Tevye saw as the reputation of a rich person is true of a person with earned degrees—"They think you really know."[3]

Finally, adolescence is detectable in student "crushes" on persons or ideas they have discovered in the resources of historical theology. This problem, which is at least as old as Corinthian fascination with Paul, Peter, and Apollos (1 Cor. 1:10–17), produces Augustinians, Thomists, Lutherans, Liberals, Fundamentalists, Barthians, Protestants, Catholics, et al. Claiming the name of Christ can even be among these distractions when chosen in dissociation from other labels. Adolescent students tend to camp around persons and ideas in a way that makes such persons and ideas ends rather than means to an end.

Coming of Age

Mark Twain once suggested that the best way to cope with a teenager is to lock him or her in a barrel with a hole in it at thirteen and plug up the hole at sixteen! Puberty and adolescence are more hopeful terms than Twain intimated. Whether biological or theological, this passage, which can so try the patience of those responsible that a "barrel" method looks attractive, leads to maturity, to coming of age.

In order for this passage to be made, exposure to the history of Christian thought must be complemented by seasoning experience in the "marketplace" and self-examining experience in the "wilderness." The marketplace is where the widely varying paths of people indiscriminately cross.[4] Primitive housing in the shadow of high-tech business, soup-lines on the same block with multimillion dollar banks, opera houses that can be seen from houses of prostitution, abortion clinics as well as neonatal nurseries, convention centers alongside hospitals for critically ill children, lavish restaurants within walking distance of single room apartments which dwellers share with rats—these contrasts illustrate the passion and the compassion, the celebration and the agony that characterize marketplace experiences. The wilderness is where identity is sought and priorities are tested.[5] Stillness replaces activism. Solitude replaces crowdedness. Reflection replaces decision-making.

The study of Christian thought requires reading books, listening to lectures, participating in group discussions, and in some cases, doing research for papers and tests. Experience in the marketplace and wilderness requires decisions, sacrifice, listening, observations, meditation, and prayer.[6] Evidence of completing a course of study in Christian history is not confusing. But what are indications of passing through "theological adolescence" into the maturity that makes this study useful for personal growth and for service?

1. *An Examined Heart*[1]

Satan cast doubt on the motive for Job's righteousness when he wondered, "Does Job fear God for nought? Hast thou not put a hedge about him and his house and all that he has, on every side?" (Job 1:9–10). Habakkuk, surrounded by the converse of his message about peace and justice, struggled to continue his prophetic mission (Hab. 1:1–4). Jesus repeatedly had to turn away from temptations with personal survival and militaristic power (Mt. 4:1–11; Jn. 6:1–15; Phil. 2:5–11). The marketplace and the wilderness test the Christian's will.

Even when obviously contradicting motives have been resolved,[8] subtle motives of the "wolf" may remain. Søren Kierkegaard wrote an "edifying discourse" about such lingering doublemindedness for conscientious worshippers and servants of God.[9] He demonstrated that those who genuinely intend to "will the good" are still vulnerable to the duplicity of willing the good for divine and/or human reward, willing the good to avoid divine and/or human punishment, willing the good "through me," or partially willing the good. Such subtle forms of doublemindedness make ministerial action conditional, reducing faithfulness to a means of self-advancement or self-defense.

In contrasting a shepherd with a hireling (Jn. 10:1–18), Jesus challenged every person intending to carry on his pastoral mission with this question, "For what or whom are you willing to die?" The statements of loyalty made by Peter and the rest of the apostles proved adolescent (Lk. 22:14–34). In the shadow of Christ's cross, they fled like hirelings. Adolescent motives tend to be self-serving. Acquiring the mind of Christ produces motives single enough to maintain integrity in spite of contradictory life situations.

2. An Honest Faith[10]

Abraham faced a lonely journey responding to God's disconcerting demand for Isaac's life (Gen. 22:1–19). Jacob wrestled with God's messengers (Gen. 32:22–32). Moses admitted his limitations as a leader (Ex. 3:11). Koheleth's caution could not keep him from assessing the suffering and injustice he saw as "grievous" and "utterly wrong" (Eccl. 2:17; 5:13). Job uncovered his frustrations with Providence. The Psalms articulate both praise and protest before God. Jesus, who refused to be called "good" in order not to eclipse the Father (Mk. 10:17–22), was doing more than being a good example in his Gethsemane prayers (Mk. 14:32–42). The marketplace and the wilderness expose the limits of finitude.

Humility must not be mistaken for paralyzing fear or demoralized retreat. Humility is the clear, honest self-understanding that results from standing, in the midst of fellow human beings, before God. Seasoned followers of Christ boldly exercise this freedom before God because their hope and confidence are anchored in the trustworthiness of God.

In the film version of *The Sound of Music*,[11] Maria repeatedly assured herself "I have confidence in me" during her journey from the abbey to the von Trapp estate. However, when she stood at the gate, she could only say, "Oh, help." Adolescent faith manifests either too little or too much caution. Acquiring the mind of Christ produces a faith strong enough to trust and honest enough to petition, "Help my unbelief."

3. A Centered Life[12]

Israel's detailed law was a commentary on its central call to covenant fidelity with the God of Abraham, Isaac, and Jacob (Ex. 19:1–6; Deut. 6:4–9). Repeatedly, Israel's prophets charged that God and his will had been forgotten (Hos. 4:1; Amos 5:21–24; Mic. 6:6–8). Nehemiah refused to be distracted by Sanballat from what he believed to be a greater responsibility (Nehemiah 4–6). When Jesus penetrated the Law and Prophets, he found their essence to be comprehensive love of God and sacrificial love of others as self (Mt. 22:34–40). He disappointed a crowd assembled to make him their king by explaining that he intended to follow, not their will, but "the will of the one who sent me" (Jn. 6:22–71). He rebuked religious leaders for perpetuating a system centered on incidentals rather than "the weightier matters" (Mt. 23:23). The marketplace and the wilderness establish theological and devotional priorities.

Good photography depends on proper focus. A good meeting hinges on following the order of business. A good book is held together by an interesting plot. A good orchestra is united by the conductor. In the same way, effective discipleship depends on a centripetal center. Schedule demands, materialistic trappings, and distracting religious issues can shackle a disciple with unhealthy points of focus. Unfortunately, this distortion can continue unchallenged for some time.

Martin Luther King, Jr.'s early experience with the Montgomery bus boycott illustrates how the marketplace and the wilderness force the issue of "centering down."[13] His northeastern theological training, his southern roots, his father's example, and his ministerial responsibilities were forced into perspective when, a few days into the boycott, he answered a midnight phone call and heard, "Nigger, we're tired of you and your mess now. If you aren't out of town in three days, we're gonna blow your brains out and blow up your house." Weary, frustrated, and fearful for his family, he told himself he had to "call on that something and person Daddy used to tell you about, the power that can make a way out of no way." He discovered that "religion had to become real to me and I had to know God for myself."

J. Wallace Hamilton tells of a strange noise that met him when he once entered his house.[14] He finally traced the noise to the sun porch where some teenage boys were playing a record into which they had drilled a hole a bit off center. Without a centering vision, adolescent theological concerns tend to produce theological sounds estranged from the heart of God. Acquiring the mind of Christ sorts out the lengthy list of possible demands and interests in terms of God and what is understood to be most important to him.

4. An Experienced Message[15]

Job, who had spoken freely at the gates about justice, had his words and integrity tested by the loss of protective hedges of blessing. The writer of Ecclesiastes struggled with wisdom and the purpose of humans in light of what he had indiscriminately observed happening "under the sun" (Eccl. 1:12–18). Jesus taught about peace when surrounded by sufferers, about justice when in sight of Roman legions and temple exploiters, and about mercy when hanging from a cross. The marketplace and the wilderness produce living echoes of God's message.

Albert Camus, in his novel *The Plague*,[16] brilliantly described through Father Paneloux the difference between a second-hand and an experienced message. A Jesuit scholar and highly placed church official, Paneloux was selected to preach in the 1940s Algerian city of Oran where bubonic plague had recently struck. Before an overflow crowd of mostly shaken inhabitants, Paneloux dramatically pressed the thesis that only the wicked should fear the plague which had been sent by God to call the wicked to repentance. Dr. Rieux, an agnostic physician faithful to his fellow human beings, was later asked by his friend Tarrou what he thought about the sermon. Dr. Rieux replied,

> I've seen too much of hospitals to relish any idea of collective punishment. But, as you know, Christians sometimes say that sort of thing without really thinking about it. They're better than they seem. . . . Paneloux is a man of learning, a scholar. He hasn't come in contact with death; that's why he can speak with such assurance of the truth—with a capital T. But every country priest who visits his parishioners and has heard a man gasping for breath on his deathbed thinks as I do. He'd try to relieve human suffering before trying to point out its excellence.[17]

A vast difference exists between a music conductor with technical skill and a music conductor in resonance with the composer(s). Similarly, an adolescent perspective on life is somewhat hollow, being based for the most part on the recycled experience of someone else. Acquiring the mind of Christ produces a perspective rooted in the context of personal experience as well as the context of Scripture.

5. A Servant Self-understanding[18]

Jesus' life was a commentary for his disciples on his teaching about service (Mt. 20:17–28; Mk. 9:35; 10:35–45). Hours before his death, Jesus left a final visual aid when he washed his closest followers' feet (Jn. 13:1–20). They did not forget the lesson (Acts 10:36–38; Gal. 6:1–10; Phil. 2:5–11; Js. 2:1–13). The marketplace and the wilderness produce servants.

Footwashing as a ceremonial act has been set aside by most Christians. Legalistically keeping such a ceremony misses the spirit in Jesus' action. However, in a culture that equates importance either with being served or with being philanthropic, engaging in periodic symbolism of a servant image through footwashing might be meaningful and revealing. Perhaps our hesitancy has less to do with an exegetical question than with the implications of the act itself. Who are legitimately called "servants"? They are those persons who can wash the feet of Christians who make them feel as if they are sitting in beds of scorpions, who can wash the feet of tradition-bound church leaders who want to keep them on a short theological leash, who can wash the feet of Christians who want highly to exalt them, who can wash the feet of the chronically ill or disabled, and who can wash the feet of those "sinners" churches and society so easily forget.

Among the many attempts to honor those who have died in battle, none is more regular than the actions at the tomb of the unknown soldier. All those otherwise forgotten are symbolically honored through the respect shown the remains of an unknown soldier. Adolescent students tend to be mesmerized by the celebrated figures in Christian history. Acquiring the mind of Christ produces a servant identity that shifts their attention to what brought these celebrated figures into prominence and that widens their cloud of witnesses to include the much larger number of the faithful who have lived and died in comparative anonymity.

Conclusion

I have hanging in my office a large frame in which pictures of several persons from Christian history who have been especially influential upon me are positioned around a print of a Grünewald painting of the crucifixion. The point: Augustine, Bernard, Erasmus, Schleiermacher, Barth, King, Bonhoeffer, Rauschenbusch, Mother Teresa, and the rest are to mediate the encounter with Christ who himself mediates the Christian's relation with God, neighbor, and self. But when does this ideal become real? When can the skills and perspectives gained in the study of historical theology become productive for personal growth and service? Perhaps the best answer is, when a person knows to ask the question. Beyond this, exposure to the history of Christian thought becomes useful when such study is complemented and followed by seasoning experience in the marketplace and self-examining experience in the wilderness.

Some are forced by traumatic life experiences to face the tests of the marketplace and to search for God in the wilderness. This has been the case for several well-known figures in modern religious thought. Such tests for Walter Rauschenbusch came by ministering to a German congregation on the corner of New York's Hell's Kitchen. For Karl Barth, by serving a Swiss congregation near the battlefields of World War I. For Mahatma Gandhi, by returning to the prejudices and oppression of South Africa and India. For Reinhold Niebuhr, by a dozen years of church work in Detroit amid the brutal effects of industrialization. For Dietrich Bonhoeffer, by a life-threatening struggle with Naziism. For Elie Wiesel, by the scars of Auschwitz and Buchenwald. For Jürgen Moltmann, by three years in World War II prisoner of war camps. For Mother Teresa, by serving the sick and dying in Calcutta.

Forced or not by circumstances that shake the very foundations for living, those who confess loyalty to Jesus Christ are led by Jesus Christ's teaching and example to locate themselves in the marketplace and the wilderness as they seek to be like him and to complete his ministry in his name. In this way, a calling is discovered in the claim, "Our creed is Christ":

To promote truth in all areas of inquiry,
To respect every human being's dignity and worth,
To follow a lifestyle that eclipses neither God nor
   neighbor,
To measure ourselves and others by the content of
   character,
To care for the weak and powerless,
To encourage artistic imagination and expression,
To keep alive the vision of freedom, peace, and justice,
To maintain a consciousness of God in all seasons, both
   of vitality and decline,
To hold vigil for the consummation of history beyond
   time.

For such persons, the study of the history of Christian

thought becomes a channel of blessing. May each reader be found among them.

Further Discussion

1. What lesson, if any, do you find in the opening observations of this chapter about Moses, Jesus, John, Timothy, and other servants of God mentioned in Scripture?

2. Do you detect (or recall) any signs of "theological puberty" in yourself?

3. Describe the "marketplace" in your life setting.

4. Where can the "wilderness" be found today? What does it mean to meditate?

5. To what do you hear Jesus refer when he points to the "wolf" in some people? Can a person remain loyal to God "for nought"? For what are you ready to sacrifice and even die?

6. What does it mean to be humble?

7. Quakers speak of "centering down." What is the center for the Christian experience? How does "centering down" come about?

Notes

[1]See Dietrich Bonhoeffer's discussion of "conformation" in his *Ethics*, ed. Eberhard Bethge, trans. Neville Horton Smith (New York: Macmillan Co., 1965), pp. 63–119.

[2]Helmut Thielicke, *A Little Exercise for Young Theologians*, trans. Charles L. Taylor (Grand Rapids, Mich.: Eerdmans, 1972). See also Augustine, *Confessions*, trans. Vernon J. Bourke (New York: Fathers of the Church, 1953); Georges Bernanos, *The Diary of a Country Priest*, trans. Pamela Morris (Garden City, N.Y.: Carroll & Graf Publishers, 1983); Dietrich Bonhoeffer, *Letters and Papers from Prison*, enlarged ed., ed. Eberhard Bethge (New York: Macmillan Co., 1972); E. L. Mascall, *Theology and the Gospel of Christ: An Essay in Reorientation*

(London: SPCK, 1977); Reinhold Niebuhr, *Leaves from the Notebook of a Tamed Cynic* (New York: Harper & Row, 1980); Michael Quoist, "Prayers on the Way of the Cross," in *Prayers*, trans. Agnes M. Forsyth and Anne Marie de Commaille (New York: Avon Books, 1975), pp. 149–79; and Landon Saunders, *Abilene Christian College 21st Annual Lectures on Preaching*, 6 lectures, 4–7 October 1971 (cassette).

[3]Joseph Stein, *Fiddler on the Roof*, Pocket Book ed. (New York: Simon & Schuster, 1971), p. 26.

[4]The writer of Ecclesiastes knew life "under the sun." Habakkuk preached peace and justice in streets controlled by violence and injustice. Jesus spent so much time in the marketplaces that crowds learned to gather there in anticipation of his arrival (Mk. 6:53–56).

[5]Among the servants of God in Scripture who were acquainted with the wilderness, see the recollections about Moses (Ex. 2:11–3:6), David (1 Samuel 16–31; Psalms 23; 51; 55), Jeremiah (Lamentations), John the Baptist (Matthew 3), Jesus (Mt. 4:1–11; 16:13–28; 17:1–8; 26:36–46), and Paul (Romans 7; Gal. 1:11–24).

[6]The French priest Michel Quoist stands out among the many persons who have prodded me toward living in the two worlds of the marketplace and the wilderness. See Neville Cryer, *Michel Quoist: A Biography* (London: Hodder & Stoughton, 1977). In the following notes, reference will be made to several of the prayers from his devotional classic *Prayers*, trans. Agnes M. Forsyth and Anne Marie de Commaille (New York: Avon Books, 1975; hereafter cited as Quoist).

[7]Quoist, "I Like Youngsters," pp. 3–5; "Lord, I Have Time," pp. 96–99; "Lord, Deliver Me from Myself," pp. 111–15; "Nothing, I am Nothing," pp. 124–26; and "Temptation," pp. 131–33.

[8]E.g., the greed of Balaam (Numbers 22–31) and Ananias and Sapphira (Acts 5:1–11), the selfish desires of David for Bathsheba (2 Samuel 11–12), the honor sought by Jesus' disciples (Mt. 18:16–22), the power bargained for by Simon Magus (Acts 8:14–24), and the envy behind some of Paul's fellow preachers of the gospel (Phil. 1:12–18).

[9]Søren Kierkegaard, *Purity of Heart Is to Will One Thing*, trans. Douglas V. Steere (New York: Harper & Row, 1948).

[10]Quoist, "The Priest, A Prayer on Sunday Night," pp. 64–68; "I Spoke, Lord," pp. 69–71; and "Help Me to Say 'Yes'," pp. 120–23. See also Søren Kierkegaard, *Fear and Trembling* and *The Sickness unto Death*, trans. Walter Lowrie (Princeton, N.J.: Princeton University Press, 1954).

[11]Richard Rogers and Oscar Hammerstein II, *The Sound of Music* (Farmington Hills, Mich.: Argyle Enterprises and Twentieth Century-Fox, 1965).

[12]Quoist, "I Would Like to Rise Very High," pp. 13–16; "Eyes," pp. 47–50; "There Are Two Loves Only," pp. 100–104; "All," pp. 105–7; and "Lord, You Have Seized Me," pp. 141–44. See also Bernard of Clairvaux, *St. Bernard on the Love of God*, trans. Terence L. Connolly (Westminster, Md.: Newman Press, 1951), and Thomas R. Kelly, *A Testament of Devotion* (New York: Harper & Row, 1941).

[13]Martin Luther King, Jr., Speech delivered in Chicago, Ill., Sept. 1966, on *In Search of Freedom*, Mercury Recording Corp. SR 61170.

[14]J. Wallace Hamilton, *Serendipity* (Old Tappan, N.J.: Fleming H. Revell Co., 1965), pp. 101–2.

[15]Quoist, "I Found Marcel Alone," pp. 54–56; "The Delinquent," pp. 57–60; "That Face, Lord, Haunts Me," pp. 72–76; "Hunger," pp. 77–80; "Housing," pp. 81–83; and "The Hospital," pp. 84–86.

[16]Albert Camus, *The Plaque*, trans. Stuart Gilbert, Vintage Books (New York: Random House, 1972).

[17]Ibid., pp. 118–19.

[18]Quoist, "Son, I Beseech You, Don't Sleep Any More," pp. 6–10; "The Funeral," pp. 40–43; and "Lord, Why Did You Tell Me to Love?" pp. 116–19.

Subject Index

Abelard: 20, 45 (n. 63)

Allegory: 2, 19

Anabaptist Thought: 21, 32

Anglican Thought: 6; William Temple, 14 (n. 21)

Anselm of Canterbury: 20, 46 (n. 74)

Apostolic Christian Thought: 1–8

Aquinas: 9, 15 (n. 23), 20

Aristotelian Thought: 9, 18, 20, 43 (n. 47)

Augustine: 9, 13 (n. 13), 15 (n. 23), 19, 43 (n. 48), 71 (n. 2)

Authority: 4–6

Baptism: 2; infant, 44 (n. 53)

Barth, K.: 9, 13 (n. 7), 41 (n. 39), 43 (n. 48), 69–70

Bauer, W.: 45 (n.66)

Bernanos, G.: 71 (n. 2)

Berdyaev, N.: 16 (n. 33)

Bernard of Clairvaux: 20, 69, 73 (n. 12)

Bonaventure: 20

Bonhoeffer, D.: 46 (n. 73), 60 (n. 4), 69–70, 71 (n. 2)

Bornkamm, G.: 41 (n. 40)

Brunner, E.: 41 (n. 39), 60 (n. 6)

Brown, Colin: 15 (n. 23)

Bultmann, R.: 9, 15 (n. 23), 16 (n. 33), 41 (n. 39)

Calvin, J..: 13 (n. 13)

Camus, A.: 12 (n. 2)

Centered life: 66–67

Centuries of Magdeburg: 21

Christendom: 5, 19–21

Christianity, essence of: 1–2, 9, 26, 48–49, 53–54

Clement of Alexandria: 13 (n. 12), 18

Clement of Rome: 18

Cobb, J.: 33

Communion: 2

Cone, J.: 15 (n. 24)

Confessing Church: 9, 14 (n. 21)

Confession: 2

Constantine: 5, 19

Conzelmann, H.: 42 (n. 40)

Councils: Chalcedon, 3; Constantinople, 2; introduction of, 19; Nicea, 2; Trent, 9; Vatican II, 9

Cullmann, O.: 14 (n. 15)

Culture: 4–5

Cyprian: 16 (n. 28), 18

Daniélou, J.: 45 (n. 59)

Deistic Thought: xv, 32

Demon Possession: 29–30

Discipleship: xix (n. 4), 49–52, chapter 4

Dodd, C. H.: 11 (n. 1)

Dolan, J.: 45 (n. 59)

Dostoyevsky, F.: 12 (n. 2)

Eastern Orthodox Thought: 6

Ebeling, G.: 41 (n. 40)

Ecclesiastical Annals: 21

Education: xiv, xix (n. 4), 1, 20–21

Enlightenment: xiv–xv, xviii (n. 3), 3, 7, 21–23, 34, 40 (n. 32)

Epicureanism: 18

Erasmus: 14 (n. 22), 21, 45 (n. 63), 69

Eusebius of Caesarea: 19

Exitentialism: 2, 7, 23

Experience: xviii (n. 1), 10, 69–70

Facts: 25

Ferguson, E.: 13 (n. 9)

Fiddler on the Roof: 8, 44, (n. 54), 57, 64

Fischer, David: 45 (n. 41), 45 (n. 62), 46 (ns. 71, 72)

Florovsky, G.: 14 (n. 19)

Fosdick, H. E.: 9, 16 (n. 26)

6:33 (51)
7:1–5 (51, 52)
7:12 (31, 51)
7:21–28 (52)
16:13–28 (72, n. 5)
16:24–26 (62)
17:1–8 (72, n. 5)
18:16–22 (72, n. 8)
20:17–28 (68)
22:34–40 (2, 48, 66)
23 (56)
23:23 (67)
24 (7)
25:31–46 (50, 52)
26:36–46 (72, n. 5)

Mark
6:53–56 (56, 72, n. 4)
9:35 (68)
9:38–41 (50, 52)
10:17–22 (66)
10:35–45 (68)
14:32–42 (66)

Luke
10:25–37 (50, 52)
18:9–14 (52)
22:14–34 (66)

John
6 (62)
6:1–15 (65)
6:22–71 (67)
8:32 (54)
10:1–18 (65)
13:1–20 (68)
14:6 (54)
14:17 (54)
17 (50, 54)

Acts
5:1–11 (72, n. 8)
7 (11)
8 (4)
8:14–24 (72, n. 8)
10:1–23 (52)
10:36–38 (68)
15 (52)
17 (11)

Romans
2:1–29 (52)
7 (72, n. 5)
8:12–30 (62)
9 (53)

9–11 (52)
12:1–2 (62)
14 (52, 52)
14:1–15:13 (52)

First Corinthians (7)
1:10–17 (64)
9:22 (54)
12:12–26 (50, 53)

Second Corinthians
5:17–21 (48)

Galatians
1:11–24 (72, n. 5)
2:1–21 (52)
2:5 (49)
2:11 (49)
3:26–28 (48, 50)
4:19 (62)
6:1–10 (68)

Ephesians
2:11–22 (48, 53)

Philippians
1:12–18 (72, n. 8)
2:1–11 (62)
2:5–11 (50, 65, 68)

Philemon
15–17 (50)

Hebrews
11 (2)
12:1–2 (50)

James
2:1–13 (52, 68)

First Peter (7)
2:18–25 (62)
5:6–11 (2)

Second Peter
3:4 (7)

First John
1:1–3 (48)
5 (64)

Revelation (6–7)
2–3 (59)
3:14–22 (50)